AF707415

Benoît Journé · Hervé Laroche ·
Corinne Bieder · Claude Gilbert
Editors

Human and Organisational Factors

Practices and Strategies for a Changing World

Editors
Benoît Journé
IAE Economie et Management
Université de Nantes
Nantes, France

Hervé Laroche
ESCP Europe
Paris, France

Corinne Bieder
Ecole Nationale de l'Aviation Civile
Toulouse, France

Claude Gilbert
Institut d'Etudes Politiques
CNRS
Grenoble, France

https://doi.org/10.1007/978-3-030-25639-5

Foreword

The industrial partners of the Foundation for an industrial safety culture (FonCSI) are convinced of the importance of considering human and organisational factors (HOF) for safety. Many companies are keen for them to be considered in their industrial safety policy, albeit at different paces. However, some issues remain unclear, the first one being that, depending on their context, companies can face difficulties in defining the notions of HOF and industrial safety. Beyond this observation, many questions are asked regarding which HOF strategies to implement, and for what purpose.

What are the concepts, the approaches by discipline and the professions (ergonomists, human factors specialists, sociologists, etc.) that need to be mobilised? How can a HOF approach to industrial safety be structured in a large group? Should it be centralised or organised according to the specific features of activities and local contexts? How should the role of HOF experts be organised? How can the extent of the company's inclusion of HOF be evaluated? What are the indicators that allow the degree of maturity and the progress needed to be measured?

This collective book is the fruit of the reflexions and debates of the third 'strategic analysis' conducted by the Foundation for an industrial safety culture. The project was simply entitled 'Human & organisational factors in high-risk companies' and sought to provide FonCSI's industrial partners with high-level research results within a limited time. The book notably presents the very valuable contributions of international experts who were invited to expose and confront their viewpoints during a 2-day residential seminar, the highlight of the strategic analysis, that was held in January 2018. The book explores the questions raised above with an emphasis on examples and lessons learned based on the field experience of its authors who come from different academic disciplines and various industrial sectors such as oil and gas, energy and transportation. It then offers some ways forward for a better consideration of human and organisational factors in hazardous companies with a view to promoting safety and facing the challenges of a rapidly changing world.

Toulouse, France FonCSI

Contents

What Is the Place of Human and Organisational Factors in Safety?

An Introduction

Claude Gilbert

Abstract It has been largely accepted, in academia as well as in business, that the main vulnerabilities in industrial safety come from human and organisational factors. Despite this consensus, it is still difficult for human and organisational factors (HOF or OHF) to become a priority within companies. There are many reasons for this: HOF are only included on the agenda in exceptional circumstances; the often-marginal position of bodies in charge of HOF, which in addition, is still a fairly heterogenous field of knowledge. Thus, the main question that seems to be raised is that of the place that should be held by HOF, with two main options: either overtly affirming their specific nature or being unobtrusively present in various ways in daily activities. In turn, this leads us to ask ourselves about the relationship between the ordinary and the exceptional within companies.

Keywords HOF · Safety · Ordinary daily life · Exceptional circumstances

The place of human and organisational factors (HOF) or organisational and human factors (OHF) in safety, notably industrial safety, is rather paradoxical. On the one hand, this question has been widely explored in the various fields of intellectual output (by academics, experts, consultants, etc.) and recognised as being important by stakeholders in safety (companies, supervisory bodies and agencies, insurance companies, etc.). On the other hand, the question would appear to be the subject of continued discussion and, although taken into account, would still not appear to be a priority.

The result of this is a hiatus between the proclamations around HOF and their veritable integration within companies and organisations responsible for managing industrial risks. This book looks beyond the injunctions that are so commonly made by academics and experts and seeks to better understand the reasons for and the implications of such a situation and then, by doing so, offer suggestions for improving it.

C. Gilbert (✉)
CNRS/FonCSI, Grenoble, France
e-mail: Claude.Gilbert@univ-grenoble-alpes.fr

B. Journé et al. (eds.), *Human and Organisational Factors*,
SpringerBriefs in Safety Management,
https://doi.org/10.1007/978-3-030-25639-5_1

1 What Place Is Given to HOF in Industrial Safety?

The way HOF are taken into account is the result of the obstacles encountered when analysing events (incidents, near-misses, accidents), which were mainly, and sometimes only, examined from a technical angle. In contemporary safety analyses, it now seems to be taken for granted that the main vulnerabilities are related to HOF, rather as if, in the various areas, we had reached the limit of the progress that could be made from a technical point of view. Thus, any significant steps forward would now have to be made at the human and at the organisational (or managerial) level. On this point, there would appear to be a fairly broad consensus which allows the engineering world to consider any residual imperfections in safety to be outside of their scope of application. This allows the world of human and social sciences (HSS) to acquire greater legitimacy for their work in this area.

However, the scope of HOF has not been clearly set out. The hesitation between HOF and OHF, which is still commonplace, is related to ongoing debates about the respective importance of "humans" and "organisations" in factors that put safety at risk. Going beyond the set-piece and spontaneous approaches around "human failings" and the progress made from the notion of "human error", the challenge is in fact to know just how far it is possible to scale the ladder of causes in order to identify or allocate responsibilities. In other words, how can we avoid limiting analysis to the behaviour of operators, or first-line management (as is still often the case)?

A number of disciplines have been drawn together to analyse HOF (ergonomics, psychology, sociology of work, management sciences, sociology of organisations, sociology of professions, etc.). Thus, knowledge capital and know-how exist, although it would still be worthwhile questioning their constitution (such as, for example, the role of human and organisational factors in the technical and scientific choices within companies?). Or, to put it another way, is the way in which HOF are limited closely related to the disciplines that have analysed them?

Nevertheless, HOF have acquired a status in the analysis of industrial safety, and companies in charge of high-risk activities have been incited to examine this issue, design specific safety actions and put in place the corresponding training. But this rather indisputable general movement is facing a number of obstacles, partly due to the fact that HOF are an "intermittent" priority within companies, according to circumstances and contexts. As a result, it is mainly when serious incidents, accidents or catastrophes occur that the debate around these factors is rekindled. Similarly, it is mainly in these circumstances that researchers, experts and actors expressing their concerns within companies are able to underline the importance of HOF.

2 HOF in Industrial Safety: Still Trying to Find their Place?

A first difficulty in the recognition of HOF comes from the fact that decision makers only take them truly into account in exceptional circumstances. Which, of course, makes regular and lasting inclusion of these questions a problem.

A second difficulty, which is related to the previous one, is that under normal circumstances, the actors in charge of HOF often hold low-profile or even marginal positions within companies. Of course, situations vary from one company to another, but these actors usually operate within specific departments, hubs or agencies, away from the major management teams. The consequence of this is that these structures, in their various positions, can appear atypical compared to the organisation as a whole, and refer to functions that need to be regularly justified and defended.

A third and final major difficulty encountered by HOF is that it is a very diverse subject. HOFs cannot be described as being a uniform topic. Although some approaches and schools are more developed than others, there is still broad heterogeneity in academic output as well as in its circulation via expert input and consultancy work. Even if, within companies, specialist HOF structures can be identified (see above), it is undeniable that questions about these factors are present in many regular activities (concerning productive performance, motivation systems, produce usage, health and safety, etc.). Thus, we find a fragmented set of references to HOF in various company departments (production, human resources, safety, etc.). Sometimes, even the actors directly confronted with safety problems "do HOF without knowing it" or, rather, without feeling the need to refer to any formal knowledge to embark on actions in this area.

For all these reasons, the place that HOF and those who promote it can have within companies is not automatic: it remains largely a work in progress. In many ways, this may seem surprising given the now-recognised importance of HOF in safety issues. We could even think that, in fact, it would not take much for HOF to be on the agenda outside of exceptional circumstances, for the issue to be addressed within companies, so that as a result of knowledge being tested on a large scale, doctrines are established and then widely shared. And yet, this is not the case, the "means of existence" of HOF remains a problem.

3 How to Make HOF "Exist"?

This question has progressively become more central in the discussions between researchers and researcher-practitioners participating in this book. The question is to decide what is the best strategy for ensuring that HOF become a lasting subject of interest within companies.

A first option is to try to make HOF a priority for safety. This is a difficult but not impossible goal to reach given the increasing attention paid to the risk of accidents, notably major ones, and the sensitivity of certain key decision makers about this subject. But this implies that those in charge of HOF would undertake very deliberate actions with great consistency over time, while associating themselves closely with the knowledge generators in this area. They would notably be raising the profile of the structures they are leading high enough for them to be heard by deciders. This option, which in many ways would appear justified, requires a lot of energy and its success is heavily dependent on the circumstances.

Another more modest and more pragmatic option is based around the idea that HOF are unlikely to be recognised as a priority by all decision makers anyway (other than the group of those who were immediately convinced by them). In this approach, the strategy would focus less on preaching their virtues and rather seek ways to allow them to become part of the ordinary daily lives of companies. In other words, to keep these concerns "alive" through a number of activities, without them being necessarily linked to any risks. The downside of this being, of course, that the question of HOF becomes less visible and less specific.

There is a debate around these two main options. The first and most obvious one is risky, in the sense that it assumes that taking into account HOF means that there is a real programme, of both knowledge and action, with true continuity over time. This has the merit of coherency and makes it possible to envisage the drafting of a doctrine based on specific knowledge and actors able to put them to the test in their activities. The second option is risky in the sense that it can lead to a certain dispersal or dilution in HOF knowledge. However, it has the merit of, discreetly and quietly, being able to penetrate all levels of the company, at various moments.

This book discusses this difficulty in finding the right position. The position is an essential question in order to determine how, today, industrial safety can be truly enriched by the learnings from work on HOF. In some ways, this then leads us to reflect on the relationship between the ordinary and the exceptional within companies managing high risk activities.

Accounting for Differing Perspectives and Values: The Rail Industry

Brendan Ryan

Abstract This chapter reflects on how researchers have worked in different ways with industry in five research projects, investigating and implementing solutions for problems related to human and organisational factors (HOF). Three observations are presented on how improvements can be made in the management of HOF.

Keywords Railway · Organisational and inter-organisational relationships · Roles of researchers and managers

1 Introduction

We often think that our own view is the best one, though there are many different perspectives of work, the workplace and organisations. People in different roles, levels of management, business functions or disciplines (e.g. safety, human factors, human resources, management science) have interests in the management of human and organisational factors (HOF).[1] Safety is often explained as a priority, but other factors (such as financial costs, production statistics, customer satisfaction) can be priorities for some people. Attention can focus on control of obvious problems (e.g. accidents during normal operations), though a narrow focus can allow vulnerability to threats from less common issues, or those that are hard to solve, especially in complex contexts, with involvement of multiple organisations.

This chapter is structured around three observations, more specifically, steps or strategies that can be considered to improve the management of HOF. These have been identified from reflection on a selection of railway research projects carried out at the University of Nottingham. The observations are as follows: (i) that there is a

[1]Human and organisational factors (HOF) as discussed in this chapter are considered to be synonymous with ergonomics and human factors (E/HF), as defined by the IEA—https://www.iea.cc/whats/.

B. Ryan (✉)
University of Nottingham, Nottingham, UK
e-mail: Brendan.Ryan@nottingham.ac.uk

B. Journé et al. (eds.), *Human and Organisational Factors*,
SpringerBriefs in Safety Management,
https://doi.org/10.1007/978-3-030-25639-5_2

lack of clarity on how HOF should be managed alongside other business objectives; (ii) that there is a need to look again at the respective roles of researchers and managers in research and practice in HOF; (iii) that HOF can be viewed as a method or analysis tool to understand the reality of people at work or interacting with systems.

2 The Research Studies

Overviews of the five projects that have informed the observations on the management of HOF are given in the Tables 2.1, 2.2, 2.3, 2.4 and 2.5.

Table 2.1 Overview of research project 1

What do people do on the railway?	
Part A	The first piece of work supported the infrastructure manager in understanding their processes for rail engineering work [23], including observing engineering work sites, interviews with staff in various roles, and group meetings to develop, display and discuss typical working scenarios (e.g. [18]). This produced an in-depth understanding of work functions and risks, descriptions of contexts and human factors affecting performance of functions. Even though we identified thematic areas and recommended programmes of work to tackle these, we were not always successful in engaging with the client and there was a perception that this was not solving the problems quickly enough
Part B	The second study was carried out for the European Union Agency for Railways (ERA), who wanted to overcome perceived bias in the industry towards technical standards [14]. This focused on what people do in a wider range of frontline railway roles (driving, rail control, station dispatch, rolling stock maintenance, infrastructure engineering). This was important in identifying: different types of *organisational* and *individual goals*; what people need to do (i.e. the *human functions*) in various *contexts*; and the *safety relevant activities* associated with these human functions

Table 2.2 Overview of research project 2

Improving safety performance in the construction supply chain	
Context	In road/rail transport construction, projects are usually conducted by multiple organisations. Evaluating the success of interventions in this type of dynamic, multi-organisational context is not straightforward. Consequently, effective evaluation studies are often not carried out
Part A	21 interviews across the supply chain explored factors affecting leadership in multi-organisation projects [21]. 26 different examples of safety leadership have been identified, aligned with nine areas from literature (e.g. demonstrating safety as a top priority, enabling safety reporting)
Part B	The effectiveness of a suite of leadership interventions is being explored in a longitudinal study in six large engineering projects. Progress (what is being implemented and how) is being tracked using theory of change methodology [7] to make sense of the wide-ranging data

Table 2.3 Overview of research project 3

What do business leaders want?	
Context	It is not known whether industry decision-makers talk naturally about safety concepts from literature (e.g. top down/bottom up safety approaches, how different forms of risk can be addressed, the nature of communications, and resilience) or how these are useful to managers
Part A	25 in-depth interviews were carried out with rail industry leaders [12], to determine what senior executives/managers really want in relation to safety and business performance. The interviews provide insight to what leaders think about trade-offs involving safety, organisational structure, the desire for improvement and the challenges in implementing changes across the industry
Part B	Two business change programmes are also being tracked over an extended period. Research activities (interviews with programme managers, review of project documents and meetings, surveys and observational work with frontline staff) are collecting broad ranging data on the programmes and safety and business performance [11]. Emerging findings indicate that industry leaders have a good awareness of problems with implementation of change programmes

Table 2.4 Overview of research project 4

Railway suicide—A continuing threat to safety and performance on the railway	
Context	There are many known prevention methods for railway suicide, but there have been few efforts to evaluate their effectiveness [16]
Part A	A collaborative project between academic researchers and industry [16], developed and implemented a method to identify the most promising safety interventions for field testing
Part B	One of the promising fencing interventions has been evaluated over an extended period of time [25]. Detailed, descriptive data are being collected on the extent of implementation and the impacts of the safety intervention. Understanding the context into which the intervention is placed has been critical
Part C	A simple evaluation framework has been developed in conjunction with the industry to support the collection of better evidence on the effectiveness of various types of safety prevention measures [17]. In spite of engagement with the industry throughout the development process, difficulties were experienced when piloting the framework with industry partners. Very simple barriers hindered progress (e.g. lack of time, not knowing where to start collecting data)

Table 2.5 Overview of research project 5

Developing new lighting products for stations	
Context	This is an innovation project, led by an industry partner, with researchers working closely with industry to provide the underpinning theory and research support. The project considers: What characteristics or qualities of lighting (e.g. movement, intensity, colour) could influence behaviour (wayfinding and crowd movement)?
Part A	Review of state-of-the-art in lighting and stakeholder engagement to support the specification and design of new lighting products for stations
Part B	Evaluation of the effectiveness of new products (using human factors methods and new sensing technologies)

3 Observations on the Management of HOF

The projects had different aims and contexts, though some overlap in their focus. There is commonality in the methods, but also differences in their application. The three observations introduced initially in Sect. 1, are expanded below.

3.1 *The Lack of Clarity on How HOF Should Be Managed Alongside Other Business Objectives*

There are multiple goals (organisational and personal—Project 1, [14]) and different objectives that can take precedence in different situations and contexts [23]. The extent to which objectives such as safety and business performance can or should compete is not clear. The interviews with business leaders (Project 3) collected views on their priorities. It is too simplistic to view these as two-way trade-offs (e.g. cost vs. safety). In practice, there are likely to be inter-changeable priorities, from amongst two or more objectives. The importance of context in trade-offs needs to be recognised.

A second consideration is that many commercial ventures are conducted by an array of organisations for a defined period. There are opportunities for leadership interventions and supply chain management to influence processes and organisational practices along the supply chain (Project 2), but to date there has been little research in this area. Units in the supply chain should not be viewed as static or homogenous entities. There will be pockets of culture in organisations and variation in behaviours within an organisation, due to the relationships and influences in multi-organisational projects.

Survivability can be considered at the heart of organisational decision-making in many circumstances. Supply chain logic indicates that organisational transition can be expected over time from survival to growth [5]. As HOF scientists and practitioners, it is important to support transitioning from a goal of survivability of the organisation to one of fulfilment of organisational needs. This can include continued efforts to raise the prominence of safety and related factors and ensure that these receive appropriate consideration alongside other objectives.

It is clear that scientists need to work with industry to be able to understand the nature of the business trade-offs as a first step in determining organisational priorities in a transitory multi-organisational context. This could include providing the tools to specify and work with data from industry and providing descriptions of the contexts and situations in which these trade-offs can occur. Doing this within a truly collaborative environment is desirable, though this is rarely achieved in practice. The respective roles of two of the stakeholders (researchers and users of HOF research, e.g. managers, practitioners, [3]) are considered in more detail below.

3.2 *Looking Again at the Roles of the Researcher and Manager*

In our projects, there were differences in the roles of the researchers and how they interacted with industry, potentially impacting on the success of the project. Implementation of a solution from academic or industry-based research is not a straightforward exercise. We have learned by experience about what can help build and inhibit collaboration in projects, such as differences in the motivations, experience, knowledge and expectations of ourselves and the other stakeholders.

In Project 1 we worked closely with industry over extended periods in the early, data gathering phase, but we could not maintain this type of collaboration through all of the research and implementation phases. We encountered similar problems in sustaining engagement in Project 4. What may appear to be good fortune (an insider researcher, [1]) facilitated access to interviews with senior decision-makers in Project 3, identifying different perspectives within and between organisations. Here the role of the researcher was critical. There are advantages to the manager-researcher (insider researcher) role, such as pre-understanding of the organisation and ability to manage organisational politics [1], often achieving results that are not possible from an outsider [4]. There are also challenges, where the manager–researcher has to “reframe their understanding” of the organisation, overcome problems associated with having a dual role [1] and various ethical issues [4].

Considering how to improve collaboration between researchers and operational staff is not a new question. Churchman and Schainblatt [2] reported that science and management need to know each other better. However, achieving “mutual understanding” [2], which is really at the heart of this problem, is not a simple endeavour. One explanation for this is that managers and scientists are not open about their real methods (e.g. how managers make decisions, or how researchers work creatively, [2]).

The researcher/practitioner gap has been explored in the discipline of ergonomics/human factors [19], pointing out problems of accessibility and usability of some academic methods. There has been reluctance to “give away” ergonomics methods to industry/novices [20], because of a required level of knowledge/expertise for the reliable and valid application of the methods. These findings on the utility of methods are important, but the interface between these groups needs closer scrutiny, to develop better collaborative work programmes. Reid et al. [15] have suggested that there is a bi-directional relationship, considering how to move ergonomics concepts from research to practice and ergonomics problems from practice to research. This is influenced by researchers (who worry about conducting “good research” for various reasons) and practitioners (who may not appreciate the value of well-designed research and feel that researchers’ interests may not align with their own).

Part of the solution to these problems is about developing better understanding of the different perspectives of those involved [15]. Whereas scientists attempt to form objective conclusions in a given set of circumstances (and at the risk of not being able to be conclusive), the manager in industry needs to make a practical decision, often in spite of uncertainty in the evidence [9]. Neumann et al. [10] have explained how generalised knowledge of science is insufficient for successful change and needs to be absorbed and combined with the existing experienced based knowledge from practitioners in organisations. Action research [10] or participatory ergonomics to embed human factors in organisations [24] are promoted as ways forward for researchers to work collaboratively with stakeholders. I have very much appreciated the analogy provided by Francois Daniellou, of the need for "researchers with dirty hands"—placing researchers on the beach with the people, rather than viewing the people from the clifftop.[2] In this analogy, researchers also need the ability to take the people to another viewpoint (e.g. mountain top). Elements of this close working with industry are evident within our projects. In Project 5, an industry partner leads the project and the motivation comes from the desire to market products. The industry is open to expertise of the researcher and potential value of scientific input. Researchers benefit from the commercial focus and clarity in priorities of the industry partners, but must be willing to be flexible and compromise, without sacrificing rigour, to reach a mutually agreeable solution.

A second set of considerations relates to the differing capabilities and limitations within these groups [3]. There are different job demands and needs across industries, and different knowledge, experience, backgrounds and education, within and between researchers and practitioners. Whilst it is right to consider the differences between research and practice, our experience indicates that there are also within group differences. As such, all partners in collaborations will lie somewhere on a continuum from pure research to pure application. We should not expect to unify or reconcile these differences and influences and the diversity has to be considered as an opportunity. We all need to reflect and be open about our weaknesses, in addition to promoting our strengths, and be receptive to new ideas and viewpoints [22] in order to find practical ways forward.

3.3 Viewing HOF as a Method or Analysis Tool to Understand the Reality of People at Work or Interacting with Systems

HOF should not just be viewed as a body of knowledge. The research projects have valued the description of work and contexts ("what people do"), usually as a part of achieving other project objectives (e.g. safety analysis or implementing and evaluating safety interventions). This description has placed an emphasis on "work as done" [8] and taken account of the wide-ranging stakeholders/organisations involved in running, maintaining or using the operational railway, and "listening to the people"

[2]Residential seminar held in January 2018 in Royaumont, France, which has led to this book (Editor's note).

at the front line to support better decision-making. It was heartening to hear that this was also recognised by the managers of organisations ("people matter more than structure", Project 3).

Our interactions with industry have also been designed to give a new view (for example using agent-based simulation, [13]), showing possibilities of what could happen. Our outputs are often in the form of simple, descriptive accounts, presenting findings from field studies in text, tables and figures. Findings can be represented in new ways, not necessarily collecting new data, but collating and compiling what already exists. This needs effort and time to do what others have not, looking again at the evidence, to make new connections in the data and help others to see what we can see. One of the challenges has been how to collate and analyse the findings in ways that are useful to both the academic and industry communities. There is a case to be made for developing better metrics and measures for the study of HOF and these are often preferred by managers and engineers. However, the value of qualitative data in research and practice is evident [6].

There are circumstances when application of our research methods needs time. For example, the evaluation studies (Projects 2, 4) and longitudinal studies (Projects 2, 3) benefit from the extended nature of these (e.g. part time Ph.D. process in some cases) and ability to track projects over lengthy time periods. This is exposing how change in business policy and practices can impact on the implementation and success of safety programmes. However, there have been situations where we have not been able to respond to the required pace of change (Project 1). We have also encountered situations where the industry has recognised how they have underestimated constraints on the speed or implications of change (Project 3). This introduces interesting questions about the existing approaches of researchers and industry staff in programmes of this nature.

4 Concluding Thoughts

The three observations offer directions for future research and practice. All work needs to operate within constraints (e.g. costs, resources, time available). However, we need to continue to promote our values and retain our disciplinary identities, especially around the importance of considering people, improving safety, life and health, otherwise we will be pushed further along routes that we do not want to go. The way of doing this is not clear, though success is likely to be found in identifying better ways to work together (especially researchers and managers), considering all business functions and all phases of exploring problems and implementing and evaluating solutions. Developing a better understanding of the different perspectives and capabilities/limitations of our partners is essential.

HOF scientists and practitioners are a body of many disciplines and backgrounds and this diversity has to be a positive thing. We need to look more carefully at the nature of our engagement and how we seek to collaborate or embed HOF in our workplaces. There have been some compelling arguments for better measures and metrics. However, we must not lose focus on collecting and articulating details of the context (i.e. looking harder, looking differently or showing others what we can see) and developing the qualitative examples and case studies that can be used in timely and practical ways by industry to start working on their immediate needs.

Acknowledgements I would like to express my thanks to all of the researchers/co-authors of the listed projects. I would also like to acknowledge and thank the many staff in industry that have supported, challenged and contributed to these projects over recent years. I also recognise the contributors at the FonCSI seminar who offered inspirational critique on the work and especially Hervé Laroche, who has provided valuable comments and input throughout the development of this chapter.

References

1. D. Coghlan, Insider action research projects. Implications for practising managers. Manag. Learn. **32**(1), 49–60 (2001)
2. C.W. Churchman, A.H. Schainblatt, The researcher and the manager: a dialectic of implementation. Manag. Sci. 11(4) (Series B, Managerial), B69–B87 (1965)
3. P.G. Dempsey, On the role of ergonomics at the interface between research and practice, in *Congress of the International Ergonomics Association* (Springer, Cham, 2018), pp. 256–263, Aug 2018
4. A. Galea, Breaking the barriers of insider research in occupational health and safety. J. Health Saf. Res. Pract. **1**(1), 3–12 (2009)
5. C. Gurău, Supply chain organization and management in French SMEs: an exploratory study, in *MEQAPS 2011 Conference*, Barcelona, Spain, 15–17 Sept 2011
6. S. Hignett, J.R. Wilson, Horses for courses—but no favourites. A reply to three commentaries. Theor. Issues Ergon. Sci. **5**(6), 517–525 (2004)
7. D. Hills, K. Junge, Guidance for transport impact evaluations. Choosing an evaluation approach to achieve better attribution, Tavistock Institute, London, UK (2010)
8. E. Hollnagel, Human factors/ergonomics as a systems discipline? The human use of human beings revisited. Appl. Ergon. **45**(1), 40–44 (2014)
9. T. Lewens, Introduction: risk and philosophy, in *Risk: Philosophical Perspectives*, ed. by T. Lewens (Routledge, Abingdon, UK, 2007)
10. W.P. Neumann, S.M. Dixon, M. Ekman, Ergonomics action research I: shifting from hypothesis testing to experiential learning. Ergonomics **55**(10), 1127–1139 (2012)
11. M. Nolan-McSweeney, B. Ryan, S. Cobb, Getting the right culture to make safety systems work in a complex rail industry, in *20th Congress of the International Ergonomics Association,* Florence, Italy, 26–30 Aug 2018
12. M. Nolan-McSweeney, B. Ryan, S. Cobb, Challenges and strategies for an effective organisational structure in a complex rail socio-technical system, in *Sixth Rail Human Factors Conference,* London, UK (2017)
13. A. Perkins, B. Ryan, P.-O. Siebers, Modelling and simulation of rail passengers to evaluate methods to reduce dwell time, in *International Conference on Modeling & Applied Simulation*, Bordeaux, France (2015)
14. L. Pickup, B. Ryan, S. Atkinson, N. Dadashi, D. Golightly, J.R. Wilson, Support Study for Human Factors Integration—Human Functions in European Railways. Report for ERA. IOE/RAIL/13/03/R, University of Nottingham (2013)
15. C.R. Reid, D. Rempel, R. Gardner, S.L. Gibson, P.G. Dempsey, C. Whitehead, Research to practice to research: part 1—a practitioner's perspective, in *Proceedings of the Human Factors*

and Ergonomics Society Annual Meeting, vol. 60, no. 1. (SAGE Publications, Los Angeles, CA, 2016), pp. 896–898, Sept 2016
16. B. Ryan, V.P. Kallberg, H. Rådbo, G.M. Havârneanu, A. Silla, K. Lukaschek, J.-M. Burkhardt, J.-L. Bruyelle, E.-M. El-Koursi, E. Beurskens, M. Hedqvist, Collecting evidence from distributed sources to evaluate railway suicide and trespass prevention measures. Ergonomics **61**, 1433–1453 (2018)
17. B. Ryan, U. Wronska, I. Stevens, Evaluating rail suicide prevention measures, in *Sixth International Rail Human Factors Conference,* London, UK (2017)
18. A. Schock, B. Ryan, J.R. Wilson, T. Clarke, S. Sharples, Visual scenario analysis: understanding human factors of planning in rail engineering. Prod. Plan. Control **21**, 386–398 (2010)
19. S.T. Shorrock, C.A. Williams, Human factors and ergonomics methods in practice: three fundamental constraints. Theor. Issues Ergon. Sci. **17**(5–6), 468–482 (2016)
20. N.A. Stanton, M.S. Young, Giving ergonomics away? The application of ergonomics methods by novices. Appl. Ergon. **34**, 479–490 (2003)
21. S. Stiles, B. Ryan, D. Golightly, Evaluating attitudes to safety leadership within rail construction projects. Saf. Sci. **110**, 134–144 (2018)
22. W. Ulrich, In memory of C. West Churchman (1913–2004) reminiscences, retrospectives, and reflections. J. Organ. Transform. Soc. Change **1**(2), 199–219 (2004)
23. J.R. Wilson, B. Ryan, A. Schock, P. Ferreira, S. Smith, J. Pitsopoulos, Understanding risk in rail engineering work systems. Ergonomics **52**, 774–790 (2009)
24. J.R. Wilson, Fundamentals of systems ergonomics/human factors. Appl. Ergon. **45**, 5–13 (2014)
25. U. Wronska, B. Ryan, Using contextual information in the evaluation of the effectiveness of mid-platform fencing, in *Sixth International Rail Human Factors Conference*, London, UK (2017)

Safety Leadership and Human and Organisational Factors (HOF)—Where Do We Go from Here?

Kathryn J. Mearns

Abstract Investigations into major disasters in safety critical industries consistently reveal failings in safety leadership, including poor decision-making and lack of effective challenge and inadequate management oversight and scrutiny of safety, as major contributory factors (e.g. Texas City, 2005; Royal Air Force Nimrod, 2006). More recently, a lack of regulatory oversight has also been implicated in disasters such as Deepwater Horizon [2] and Fukushima Daiichi [17]. There is also evidence of an inability to apply the lessons learned from major accidents, whether they have occurred in the same or other major accident hazard industries. This chapter considers these issues and the potential interplay between actors at the more senior levels of organisations and the regulators of the industries involved. The chapter also considers the role of safety culture assessments as a means of identifying the human and organisational factors that are either undermining or enhancing safety within the organisation and the need for senior leadership having the right mind-set to take due cognisance of this intelligence to implement measures that improve safety. Strong and competent regulators should support this approach.

Keywords Public inquiries · Leadership · Safety culture · Regulators

> The organizational causes of this disaster are deeply rooted in the histories and cultures of the offshore oil and gas industry and the governance provided by the associated public regulatory agencies. While this particular disaster involves a particular group of organizations, the roots of the disaster transcend this group of organizations. This disaster involves an international industry and its governance ([2], Investigation of the Macondo Well Blowout Disaster, p. 9).

K. J. Mearns (✉)
Wood PLC, Aberdeen, UK
e-mail: k.j.mearns@gmail.com

B. Journé et al. (eds.), *Human and Organisational Factors*,
SpringerBriefs in Safety Management,
https://doi.org/10.1007/978-3-030-25639-5_3

1 Introduction

The quote given at the start of this chapter highlights the human, organisational, regulatory and 'cultural' shortcomings that have been consistently identified as underlying causes of major accidents in safety critical industries, irrespective of technology or regulatory regime. The list includes Bhopal, Herald of Free Enterprise, Three Mile Island, Chernobyl, Challenger, Columbia, Texas City, Royal Air Force (RAF) Nimrod, Deepwater Horizon and Fukushima Daiichi. The common failings identified from Public Inquiries and investigations into these major disasters, include:

- Ineffective leadership;
- Poor operational attitudes and behaviour;
- Poor decision-making and lack of effective challenge;
- Lack of training and competence;
- Inadequate management oversight and scrutiny of safety;
- Failure to apply safety lessons learned both from within and outside the organisation and/or industry.

The investigations invariably identify failings at the organisational level (i.e. senior leadership), particularly regarding decisions around the production/safety trade-off. For example, in his report into the loss of the RAF Nimrod, Charles Haddon-Cave [8], referred to 'A Failure of Culture, Leadership and Priorities' and provides damning criticism of Britain's largest defense and arms company:

> The regrettable conduct of some of BAE Systems' managers[1] suggests BAE Systems has failed to implement an adequate or effective culture, committed to safety and ethical conduct. The responsibility for this must lie with the leadership of the company (p. 261).

These investigations into major disasters also consistently call for 'lessons to be learned' but it would appear that either these lessons are quickly forgotten or there is a failure to implement the necessary actions arising from these lessons. For example, the Deepwater Horizon Study Group [2] reports that:

> At the time of the Macondo blowout, BP's corporate culture remained one that was embedded in risk-taking and cost-cutting – it was like that in 2005 (Texas City), in 2006 (Alaska North Slope Spill), and in 2010 ("The Spill"), (p. 5).

BP clearly failed to implement the lessons learned from its previous disasters, as did NASA in the case of Challenger [25] and Columbia [24].

Apart from the major accident investigation findings, the research evidence shows strong support for the relationship between effective safety leadership at all management levels (including executives), a healthy safety culture and good safety performance (for reviews see [9, 10]). There is also an increasing focus on the role of regulators and their contribution to the aetiology of these disasters and a call for more competent and challenging regulators for the industries affected, i.e. offshore oil and gas (Deepwater Horizon) and nuclear industries (Fukushima Daiichi).

---

[1] BAE Systems is a British aerospace and defence large industrial group.

The objective of this chapter is not to provide a new theory or share new ideas about how to improve human and organisational factors (HOF) in safety. On the contrary, the chapter explores the evidence that we already have to demonstrate that a focus on HOF is required to improve safety and how that focus can be achieved. As a result, this chapter covers three themes:

1. The role that leadership plays in developing and sustaining the safety culture of their organisations;
2. The importance of regular assessment of and attention to safety culture to identify the state of human and organisational factors that influence safety;
3. The role of a competent regulator in the oversight of leadership and management for safety and ensuring that adequate attention is paid to the findings of safety culture assessments to inform senior management leadership and decision-making.

2 The Role of Leadership in Developing and Sustaining Safety Culture

> Perhaps there is no clear-cut "evidence" that someone in BP or in the other organizations in the Macondo well project made a conscious decision to put costs before safety; nevertheless, that misses the point. It is the underlying "unconscious mind" that governs the actions of an organization and its personnel. Cultural influences that permeate an organization and an industry and manifest in actions that can either promote and nurture a high reliability organization with high reliability systems, or actions reflective of complacency, excessive risk-taking, and a loss of situational awareness [2, pp. 5–6].

A wealth of research data has been generated on how leadership at all levels of an organisation can influence the safety performance of front-line operations. This includes research on the role of supervisors [18, 27], middle management [15, 19] and senior management [5, 20]. The role of senior management commitment to safety seems to be particularly important, in that their perceived attitudes, values and actions appear to be one of the most cited components of safety climate and safety culture research [4].

3 The Role of Safety Climate and Safety Culture Assessments

Senior managers set the agenda for safety in terms of their vision, values and strategy for safety, however this can only work if it is accepted, adopted and implemented throughout the whole organisation. Acquiring the right sort of 'safety intelligence' from the bottom up [7] is important. Managers at all levels of an organisation must be receptive to 'bad news' as well as 'good news' and they must be attentive to the 'signals' that indicate all is not well within their organisation and be willing to take action where necessary. A properly developed and implemented safety culture assessment provides a wealth of safety intelligence for managers to act upon.

Safety climate and culture assessments provide an opportunity for senior managers to gain an understanding of how the safety management systems (SMSs) and technical safety interventions as conceived and constructed are actually implemented in the organisation. There is often a mismatch between 'work as imagined' versus 'work as done' and between 'work as prescribed' versus 'work as disclosed' [3, 12]. Safety climate/culture assessments can assist in identifying where these mismatches lie and if properly conducted can identify the interventions that can close the gaps.

4 The Role of the Regulator

It is important for all employers and employees, to be aware of and fully understand, their duties under legal frameworks for health and safety. Within the UK this is enshrined in the Health and Safety at Work, etc. Act (1974) with other legislation arising from it, e.g. Management of Health and Safety at Work Regulations (1999).

More recently, the UK's Corporate Manslaughter and Homicide Act 2007, clarifies the criminal liabilities of companies where failures in the management of health and safety result in a fatality. Prosecutions are of the corporate body itself, however, directors, board members and others can still be prosecuted for separate health and safety offences. One of the challenges of the act is identifying 'the controlling mind', i.e. the person whose thoughts and actions control the company's affairs. This is particularly difficult in large companies where there are complex management structures and health and safety is often delegated to more junior managers who are not 'controlling minds'. Prosecutions therefore tend to be more successful under breaches of the Health and Safety at Work etc. Act 1974, although there have also been successful prosecutions under the Corporate Manslaughter and Homicide Act 2007 (e.g. the Lyme Bay tragedy).

Before an organisation ends up in court for serious breaches of health and safety legislation, government regulators have the power to shut down operations if they have evidence that the legislation is not being complied with. This is the sort of independent challenge that senior managers usually respect and pay attention to. It is the ultimate challenge, with severe consequences for the profitability of the organisation. If there is a fatality or major accident, the imposition of fines will hurt the company's 'bottom line'; the publicity and its consequences will hurt the company's 'reputation'. These are matters very close to any senior manager's heart. Furthermore, apart from the consequences for the organisation, there can also be consequences for the individual with many senior managers reporting they never want to be in a position to tell family members that a loved one will not be coming home following a fatal accident. Such experiences tend to develop managers who have a focus on health and safety. Fortunately, major accidents are comparatively rare events as are fatal accidents at work, so the capacity for this type of emotional learning is very limited and it could obviously never be endorsed.

In making decisions to shut down company operations, the regulator has to be 'proportionate' in its assessment with due reference to the concept of 'as low as reasonably practicable' (ALARP). This means that the regulator has to assess whether the measures taken are grossly disproportionate in relation to mitigating those risks. This trade-off has to be considered in the context of the law and what is acceptable from a risk management and safety perspective. ALARP serves society by placing a heavy weight on the precautionary principle in a way that controls risks for human beings and the environment. The practical procedures for implementing ALARP are mainly found in engineering judgements and codes but also in traditional cost-benefit analysis (CBA). According to Aven and Abrahamsen [1], CBA ignores uncertainties because it is based on attitudes to risk and uncertainty, which are 'risk neutral' and therefore in conflict with the precautionary principle and ALARP. French et al. [6] also identify shortcomings with CBA and advocate the implementation of multi-attribute utility theory (MAUT) to address the perceptions of all stakeholder groups in order to facilitate constructive discussion. They argue that being explicitly subjective provides an open, auditable and clear analysis, which contrasts with the 'illusory' objectivity of CBA. The findings from safety climate/culture assessments reflect the perceived/subjective risks of stakeholders on the front-line and throughout the wider organisation and could be used in MAUT as another tool to add to the organisation's and the regulator's armoury to assess risks and support decision-making.

If senior management are so critical to developing and sustaining an organisation's safety culture and are instrumental in assessing and managing the organisation's health and safety risks, how can we determine whether they display the necessary leadership qualities, decision-making processes, capacity to manage organisational change and learn from previous accidents?

5 A Regulatory Perspective on Leadership and Management for Safety (L&MfS)

The International Atomic Energy Agency (IAEA) has developed guidance for managers and regulators to assess L&MfS [14]. The UK Office for Nuclear Regulation (ONR) provides an example of how this guidance has been implemented. The ONR regulates the UK nuclear industry using a set of Safety Assessment Principals (SAPs) that have to be complied with before nuclear organisations in the UK can be granted a licence to operate [16]. Four Management System (MS) SAPs are key: MS.1-Leadership; MS.2-Capable Organisation; MS.3 Decision Making and MS.4 Learning. Each SAP consists of a number of components, e.g. leadership attributes; control of organisational change; decision-making processes and learning culture, etc. These four ONR SAPs and their components also make clear links to safety culture. The ONR uses these SAPs and associated guidance to conduct L&MfS reviews of duty holders as and when required. The managers of nuclear organisations have to demonstrate their competence in these areas as part of the Safety Case and Periodic Reviews of Safety (PRSs) to ensure that the company is still fit to operate.

Originally designed as a set of themes for discussions at the executive level of the organisation, the L&MfS reviews allow the regulator to challenge senior managers on their leadership, their organisational capability, e.g. knowledge management and succession planning, decision-making, and learning ability, i.e. do they learn from incidents and implement the necessary changes to prevent such an incident occurring again. This can consist of a review of an organisation's safety management system (SMS) and a series of interviews and/or focus groups with a cross-section of the organisation's workforce, including senior management. Reviews of safety culture assessments, incident investigations and operating experience reports can also be conducted. These help to demonstrate the extent to which the 'work as imagined' matches 'work as done' and 'work as prescribed' matches the 'work as disclosed'.

Other regulators, e.g. the Health and Safety Executive [11] and industry bodies e.g. International Association of Oil and Gas Producers [13] have issued safety leadership guidance. Clear guidance and strong regulatory scrutiny can provide the necessary incentive for organisational leaders and senior managers to focus on improving their own decision-making processes and behaviour and appreciate the central role they play in developing and reinforcing the safety culture within the organisations they are responsible and accountable for.

6 Conclusions

Human, organisational, regulatory and 'cultural' shortcomings have been consistently identified as underlying causes of major accidents in safety critical industries, irrespective of technology or regulatory regime. Despite this wealth of data, there is also evidence of an inability to apply the lessons learned from major accidents, whether in the same or other industries. The challenges faced by the complex (and often complicated) organisations that run safety critical industries, should not be underestimated, however the evidence from public inquiries and investigations into major accidents indicate that demonstrations of stronger regulatory oversight and an engaged and accountable senior management are worthy of consideration. Furthermore, decades of research has shown that no matter what the industry, the same issues emerge from safety culture/climate assessments, i.e. perceived lack of senior management commitment to safety; inadequate communication (too much of the wrong sort or too little of the right sort); inadequate procedures (badly written or out-of-date); inability to 'speak up'/fear of 'challenging' about safety and lack of organisational learning.

On providing senior managers with feedback from their safety culture/climate surveys, there is often disbelief that the workforce views the organisation in this way. Indeed, a common finding from these surveys is that senior managers perceive the safety culture as much more positive than their workforces. As a result, there can be a reluctance to do anything about the findings. Action plans are developed but evidence of serious implementation is not necessarily forthcoming. Senior managers are very good at talking about the importance of safety but seem less able to address the human and organisational issues that undermine safety. They also often seem to be unable to implement the lessons learned from public inquiries into major accidents, despite the findings from these inquiries being widely available. What could be the reasons for this? Is it because interventions arising from safety culture/climate findings and the findings of public inquiries into major accidents are too costly? Or is there an attitude that this could never happen here? Or do senior managers simply not understand how HOF can influence the safety performance of an organisation? Given the decades of evidence to the contrary, these reasons are not tenable and yet, no other reasons come to mind except that making profits and keeping the shareholders happy are paramount and trump all other considerations. To some extent, this is understandable. Safety cannot be sustained if the company is not making money to invest in improvements. Fortunately, major accidents are rare events and therefore the attitude 'it cannot happen here', may be justified in the minds of senior managers, however, as Trevor Kletz is famously reported as saying, '*If you think safety is expensive, try having an accident*'.

In order to make progress, safety critical industries require well-resourced and highly competent regulators who are capable of making strong and legitimate challenges to senior managers on their safety leadership qualities, backed up by enforcement action. Unfortunately, there has been a trend in recent years towards deregulation, often with drastic consequences, e.g. the 2008 financial crash, and continuing debates about whether or not the internet should be regulated. The lack of adequate regulation was also implicated in the Macondo (Deepwater Horizon) and Fukushima Daiichi disasters and a recent UK parliamentary inquiry into the collapse of the Carillion organisation, revealed evidence of weak financial and pensions regulators.

The way forward is for regulators and senior managers to work together to achieve safer and more resilient working environments in safety critical industries. However, we must not forget the workforce's involvement in this process and this is where safety climate and culture assessments play a role. These assessments provide good safety information to senior managers but only if properly developed and implemented by competent people with an understanding of the validity and reliability of their measures. Depending on the level of the analysis required, these assessments cover themes such as the lack of cross-communication, which prevents reciprocity, the validity of work systems and procedures, i.e. work as imagined and prescribed in the SMS does not reflect work as disclosed and done on the front-line, and the lack of leadership visibility to reinforce the norms and values that define the organisation. Leaders need to learn about and understand these issues by actively listening as well as observing because, as many public inquiries into major accidents have demonstrated, these are the conditions that could show that their organisation is drifting towards failure [3].

Woods [26] makes reference to the 4Is (independent, involved, informative and informed) and the need for an independent challenge of senior managers' decision making in their trade-offs between production and safety. Competent regulators can provide that independent and informed challenge along with the insights provided by properly developed and implemented safety culture/climate assessments, which ensures the involvement of the workforce in providing the information for management to act upon. These assessments can be used in the implementation of MAUT to address the perceptions of all stakeholder groups, facilitate constructive discussion and support the decision-making of senior managers and regulators.

References

1. T. Aven, E. Abrahamsen, On the use of cost-benefit analysis in ALARP processes. Int. J. Perform. Eng. **3**(3), 345–353 (2007)
2. Deepwater Horizon Study Group, *Final Report on the Investigation of the Macondo Well Blowout.* Center for Catastrophic Risk Management, Mar 2011
3. S. Dekker, Malicious compliance, in *Hindsight, Summer 2017, EUROCONTROL*, vol. 25 (2017), pp. 8–9
4. R. Flin, K. Mearns, P. O'Connor, R. Bryden, Measuring safety climate: identifying the common features. Saf. Sci. **34**(1–3), 177–192 (2000)
5. R. Flin, S. Yule, Leadership for safety: industrial experience. Br. Med. J. Qual. Saf. **13**, 45–51 (2004)
6. S. French, T. Bedford, E. Atherton, Supporting ALARP decision-making by cost benefit analysis and multi attribute utility theory. J. Risk Res. **8**(3), 207–233 (2005)
7. L.S. Fruhen, K. Mearns, R. Flin, B. Kirwan, Safety intelligence: an exploration of senior managers' characteristics. Appl. Ergon. **45**, 967–975 (2014)
8. C. Haddon-Cave QC, *The Nimrod Review. An Independent Review into the Broader Issues Surrounding the Loss of the RAF Nimrod MR2 Aircraft XV230 in Afghanistan in 2006* (The Stationary Office, London, 2009)
9. Health and Safety Executive, *The role of managerial leadership in determining safety outcomes.* Research Report 044, HM Stationary Office, Norwich (2003)
10. Health and Safety Executive, *A Review of the Literature on Effective Leadership Behaviours for Safety.* Research Report 952 (HSE Books, 2012)
11. Health and Safety Executive, *Leading Health and Safety at Work, Actions for Directors, Board Members and Organizations of all Sizes.* INDG 417 (HSE Books, 2013)
12. E. Hollnagel, Can we ever imagine how work is done?, in *Hindsight, Summer 2017, EUROCONTROL*, vol. 25 (2017), pp. 10–14
13. International Association of Oil and Gas Producers, *Shaping safety culture through safety leadership.* Report No. 452. London (2013)
14. International Atomic Energy Agency, Leadership and Management for Safety. General Safety Requirements, No. GSR Part 2, IAEA, Vienna (2016)
15. A. O'Dea, R. Flin, Site managers and safety leadership in the offshore oil and gas industry. Saf. Sci. **37**, 39–57 (2001)
16. Office for Nuclear Regulation (ONR), Safety Assessment Principles, Version 0, (2014)
17. Organisation for Economic Co-operation and Development [OECD]/Nuclear Energy Agency (NEA), *Five years after the Fukushima Daiichi Accident: Nuclear Safety Improvements and Lessons Learnt.* NEA No. 7284, (OECD/NEA Publishing, 2 rue Andre-Pascal, 75775 Paris Cedex 16, 2016)
18. T.M. Probst, Organizational safety climate and supervisor enforcement: multilevel explorations of the causes of accident underreporting. J. Appl. Psychol. **100**(6), 1899–1907 (2015)
19. Z. Rezvani, P. Hudson, Breaking the clay layer: the role of middle management in the management of safety. J. Loss Prev. Process Ind. **44**, 241–246 (2016)

20. I. Roger, R. Flin, K. Mearns, Safety leadership from the top: identifying the key behaviours, in *Proceedings of the Human Factors and Ergonomics Society 55th Annual Meeting*, Las Vegas, USA (2011)
21. UK Health and Safety Executive (HSE), Health and Safety at Work etc. Act 1974
22. UK Health and Safety Executive (HSE), Management Regulations, 1999
23. UK Ministry of Justice, Corporate Manslaughter and Corporate Homicide Act 2007
24. U.S. Columbia Accident Investigation Board (CAIB), *Report of the Columbia Accident Investigation Board*, Arlington, VA, vol. 1 (2003)
25. D. Vaughan, *The Challenger Launch Decision: Risky Technology, Culture, and Deviance at NASA* (University of Chicago Press, Chicago, 1996)
26. D. Woods, How to design a safety organization: test case for resilience engineering, in *Resilience Engineering: Concepts and Precepts*, ed. by E. Hollnagel, D. Woods, N. Levenson (CRC Press, Boca Raton, Florida, 2006)
27. D. Zohar, A group-level model of safety climate: testing the effect of group climate on micro-accidents in manufacturing jobs. J. Appl. Psychol. **85**, 587–596 (2000)

Considering Human and Organizational Factors in Risk Industries

What Should We Expect? How Do We Manage this Subject?

Christian Neveu, Valérie Lagrange, Philippe Noël and Nicolas Herchin

Abstract The industrial partners of the Foundation for an industrial safety culture (FonCSI) agree on the importance of considering human and organizational factors (HOF) for safety. Nevertheless, many questions remain regarding how to address this issue in industrial organizations. In this short chapter, HOF experts of companies supporting FonCSI and representing various industrial sectors (energy, transports, oil & gas) expose their viewpoint on HOF goals, strategies, approaches, methods and tools.

Keywords Risk management · HOF approach · Safety strategy

1 HOF Approach: Features and Benefits

Since the creation of the risk industries, different kinds of approaches have been developed in order to avoid accidents: although at first purely technical, since the 1980s these approaches have taken into account human and organizational factors (HOF) (see Fig. 1).

Today, the lessons learned from each of these historical steps show that risk industries need to implement a HOF approach with particular features:

- *an integrated approach,* distinct from the "man or machine" dichotomy;

C. Neveu (✉)
SNCF, Paris-Saint-Denis, France
e-mail: christian.neveu@laposte.net

V. Lagrange
EDF, Paris-Saint-Denis, France

P. Noël
TOTAL, Paris-La Défense, France

N. Herchin
GRTgaz, Paris-Saint-Denis, France

B. Journé et al. (eds.), *Human and Organisational Factors*,
SpringerBriefs in Safety Management,
https://doi.org/10.1007/978-3-030-25639-5_4

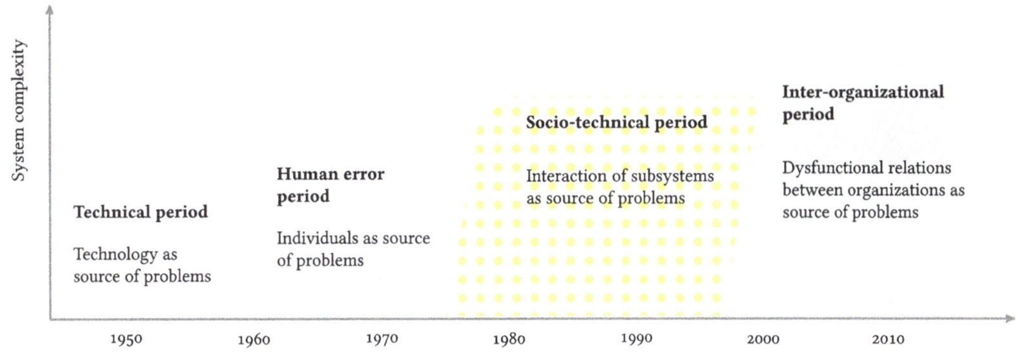

Fig. 1 Evolution of risk management approaches (adapted from [1, 2])

- *a realistic vision of the 'human'*, as a factor of reliability with limits, whose role must be facilitated by:
  - reducing the situations favourable to errors and failures,
  - reinforcing the capacity and the means to manage the diversity and the unforeseen nature of operational situations;
- *a "field" approach*, based on the interactions between technical systems, humans and organization in real situations.

For these reasons, FonCSI's definition of HOF seems to be particularly pertinent: "*identify and set up the conditions which favour a positive contribution of operators and collectives in safety*".

Furthermore, with this kind of HOF approach, even if it focuses on safety and security performances, it actually contributes more globally to the quality of operation as a whole and is positive for all performances.

Following these historical steps, such programs initially dealt with human factors in incident investigation, ergonomics in the workplace and human factors in design. Then, the influences of sociology and psychology led to research to understand problems in organizations that resulted in incidents. The issues of decision making, safety culture, management of change, cooperation, are now also taken into consideration. They concern everybody, from the operator to the senior vice-president and all managers; they concern corrective actions after incidents, but are increasingly focused on preventive actions, which form part of the initial training for individuals and of continuous improvement action plans for units (Fig. 2).

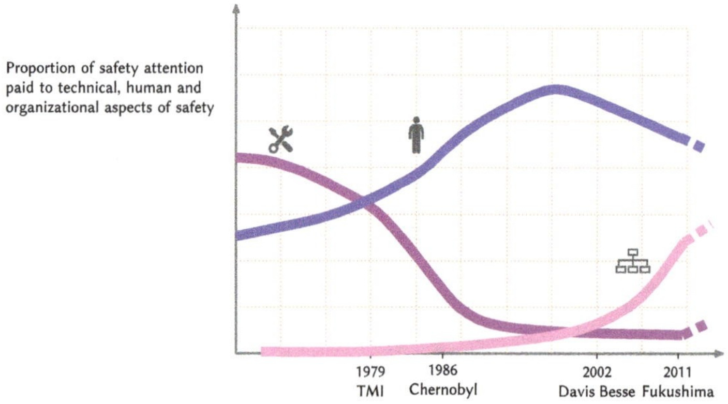

Technical reliability	After TMI Human performance	After Chernobyl Safety culture	After Davis Besse Weak signals	After Fukushima Resilience
Emphasis on robust design Quality management Defence in depth	Automation Procedural guidance Crisis management Simulator-based training Ergonomic design Onsite safety engineer Organizational factors in experience feedback	Develop questioning attitude, rigourous and prudent approach Role of managers Criticity management Internal control evaluations Onsite HF specialist	Avoid normalization of deviance Reaffirm safety culture principles Safety management guide Human perf. project Org. factors in design phase ("SOH" approach)	Adaptation to extreme situations Reaffirm defence in depth, systemic approach, safety culture Emergency responders, crisis management Safety culture approach

Fig. 2 Evolution of the attention given to the dimensions of safety management at EDF (adapted, with permission, from an internal EDF document)

2 How Do We Implement and Manage HOF Approaches?

Through the historical development of HOF approaches in risk industries—aeronautics, railways, nuclear, oil & gas… and now in the health sector, an "ideal" implementation has clearly emerged:

- It would begin by creating a team of *HOF Experts*[1] at the corporate level, in order to define a roadmap (aims and strategy for the next 3–4 years, based on a diagnosis) addressed to the top management and to suggest methods and tools for supporting the HOF dynamics.
- Then, it needs to benefit from relays in the organization, by putting in place *HOF consultants*[2] or *HOF correspondents*[3] at local levels or intermediate levels in charge of developing action plans: HOF training, field analysis, support departments and local managers for main actions such as implementing HOF methods and tools such as incident investigation, human performance, operational decision making … (Fig. 3).

[1]Expert means Ph.D. or at least 3rd cycle graduate in ergonomics, psychology, or sociology, with a position in the organization in order to support the top management in HOF domain.

[2]Consultant means a 4–5 years mission carried out by a person who may have an operational background but has received additional high-level training in HOF.

[3]Correspondent means a person well trained on one specific HOF method (short training), identified as a referent inside her/his department.

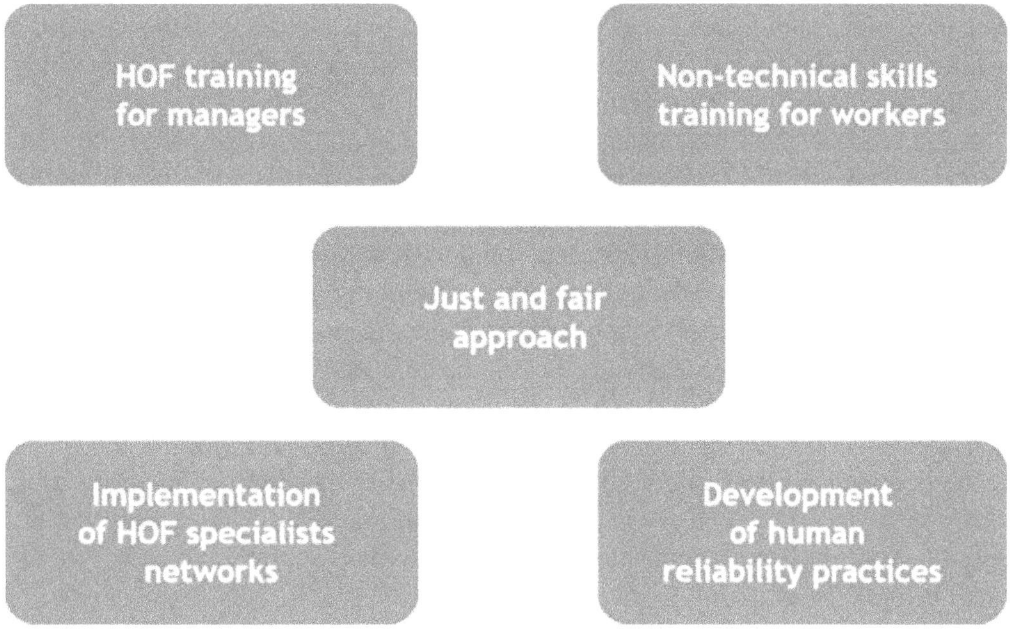

Fig. 3 Content of the SNCF HOF project

Depending on the current challenges of the company and its maturity level in this area, the implementation of the HOF approach could take various forms. Nevertheless, three invariants need to be respected:

- Whatever the methods used by companies, the effectiveness of the program relies on an in-depth understanding of functions and risks, discovering the real human activity in a job or a task. It must be focused on what people do, how safety is produced, what can go wrong and what can be done to prevent this.
- In each sector, the HOF approach must be controlled: by the safety management system (SMS), with a clear ambition, action plan, measure of performance and efficiency.
- The basis of HOF dynamics requires competencies, from experts/consultants/correspondents, but also from each employee, including managers. Everybody has to acquire HOF skills—knowledge and know-how—in order to develop a safety culture and good practices.

3 Difficulties and Opportunities

The first key problem to achieving the objectives of HOF programs observed in companies is the turnover of staff in the management line, and specifically at the senior management level. The senior management of the entity must be involved in the program as the main sponsor. This is a key condition to ensuring that it will be taken to its conclusion even though the environment may change. However, each time the senior management changes, the program runs the risk of being stopped or reinitialized, with a period of questioning. Sometimes the turnover rate is so high that the outcomes of such program are lost.

Another aspect is the continuous moving environment. The worldwide or domestic market can quickly change because of unforeseen circumstances; this could result in a decision being made to change the organization, the methods implemented and/or the tools. Because HOF programs need time to achieve their results, in a moving environment they are exposed to be defined again in order to be well-adapted.

It probably means that HOF are not really integrated enough in safety management processes. They depend to a large extent on the conviction of individuals, not of the whole organization.

The second key problem observed on how HOF programs work is the impact of the regulator which has not necessarily reached a high level of maturity in the HOF approach (e.g. looking for responsibility versus discovering the work situation). Based on how the observed reaction of the regulator is perceived, the HOF program could be influenced.

Moreover, most of the HOF programs that have been performed in companies are mainly focused on the human factors that can influence human performance: inadequate procedures, inadequate communication, inability to implement lessons learned, perceived lack of management and commitment to safety. It is still a challenge to really implement programs addressing organizational factors with inputs from sociology. When we analyse some recent big changes in organization (at corporate or site level), it is clear that companies still have to improve their ability to analyse organizational factors and customize their change program based on the results of such analyses.

Training is one of the ways of making progress. Training must cover all the employees of the organization, from the executive management to frontline workers. When most of the HOF training is integrated in the baseline competencies training program, efficiency is better. It facilitates the incorporation of HOF methods and behaviours in daily management and operational tasks. With this practice, managers strive to consider HOF methods as a further step to managing the organization, broader than safety. Frontline workers are more convinced that HOF influence their safety decisions and actions, and thus more likely to deliver safe acts.

One challenge for companies is to gather information on the tools, methods and studies that have been used with success, with the relevant agility in a moving environment. They could be established as a reference for some questions or problems that were an issue in the past and have resurfaced in another branch of the company, or sometimes, unfortunately, in the same branch.

A collection of good practices can also be made between companies, whether they are from the same sector or not.

4 As a Conclusion

According to the benchmark of the different risk industries and to the international experts' points of view,[4] we can say that a HOF approach cannot be reduced to the use of methods and tools. At the core of such an approach, a strong conviction from the top managers of the organization is required, expressed by a clear ambition (i.e. strategic vision and required means) and a strong commitment that is visible to everybody in daily decisions and behaviours.

References

1. J. Reason, Managing the management risk: New approaches to organisational safety, in *Reliability and Safety in Hazardous Work Systems: Approaches to Analysis and Design*, ed. by B. Wilpert, T. Qvale (Lawrence, Hove, 1993), pp. 7–21
2. B. Wilpert, B. Fahlbruch, Safety related interventions in interorganisational fields, in *Safety Management and the Challenge of Organisational Change*, ed. by A. Hale, M. Baram (Elsevier, Oxford, 1998)

[4] The experts that participate in the FonCSI residential seminar held in January 2018 (Editor's note).

The Key Drivers to Setting up a Valuable and Sustainable HOF Approach in a High-Risk Company such as Airbus

Florence Reuzeau

Abstract Airbus has been investing in developing human and organizational factors (HOF) approaches for the last three decades. With hindsight, we can identify and capitalize on the key drivers for setting up a valuable and sustainable HOF approach in a high-risk company such as Airbus. These drivers can be the role of regulators, the standardization and visibility of HOF approaches within the company, HOF governance and competence management. However, there is no room for complacency in a competitive market with regards to sustaining HOF approaches at the appropriate level. Therefore, the message should be to define and measure what can be described as HOF maturity indicators to be integrated into the company dashboard.

Keywords Human factors · Organizational factors · Standards · Competences · Governance · Maturity

1 Introduction

The development of human and organizational factors (HOF) approaches in a large group depends on very different factors such as the expected benefits, obligations (certification), induced cost and organizational structure of the company. In Airbus, there are two endemic issues: human factors and organizational factors.

The first issue relates to the human factors (HF) at workstation for the workers (or blue-collars) in the plants as well as for the human operators of an aircraft: reducing the effect of working conditions on the Health and Safety of human operators, enhancing the safety of air transportation, supporting the introduction of new technologies, machines, tools, or new operational procedures. Productivity and cost reduction are part of the equation, as are cost of design, industrialization and end-user training. Whatever the domain of application, the key challenge today and for the future is to understand and anticipate how human operators can behave and will

F. Reuzeau (✉)
Airbus, Toulouse, France
e-mail: florence.reuzeau@airbus.com

B. Journé et al. (eds.), *Human and Organisational Factors*,
SpringerBriefs in Safety Management,
https://doi.org/10.1007/978-3-030-25639-5_5

behave in their daily operations. This is particularly challenging for the aircraft product as they are designed to be used for around 40 years, meaning there will be two or three generations of multi-cultural human operators. Disciplines such as psychology, ergonomics, sociology, linguistics and neuroscience are fully integrated into the company to cope with these aspects.

The second issue relates to organizational factors (OF). Airbus is an international company whose research, development, production and customer services activities are distributed in Europe and around the world. How can international organizations, processes, methods and tools be conceived to be usable by any employee in order to design, produce and deliver the order backlog, taking safety, security and profitability into account? In addition, company performance is subject to the performance of the whole extended enterprise, the suppliers and the subcontractors. Moreover, there is some internal testing of new organizational ways of working such as liberated enterprise, agile methodology, remote work. It is very difficult in such an organization to differentiate the implications of individual versus collective factors on the work.

Management sciences, psychologists and sociologists from Human Resources are supporting these actions in a transnational mode. It is quite a new phenomenon compared to the introduction of human sciences in the human factors field.

2 History, Looking Back

Airbus historically invested in HOF approaches in industrial production mainly for Health & Safety considerations. In 1984, the first “ergonomics department” was set up in the manufacturing organization to develop “work analysis” as a key methodology for supporting the introduction of new and novel machines, tools, product lines and new buildings. This included working organization, job instructions, training, etc. In 1993, the decision was made to allocate one ergonomist position per plant and assembly line to support management decision-making. The great diversity of human factors issues (physical ergonomics, cognitive ergonomics, health, mixed workers generation, competences, robots/cobots, and new technologies like augmented reality, etc.) and the chasing of human-induced non-quality make this job quite challenging. Today, the company is engaged in the digital transformation through the factory of the future. Airbus mandated an ergonomist coordinator to gather and share best practices among the facilities distributed in Europe.

In 1988, the Airbus Training Center was also provided with a small team of people with human factors competences in charge of developing and deploying teaching techniques and working with instructors to define training policies (in line with the Crew Resource Management courses).

Early 1990s, it was decided to set up a new HF organization for supporting the commercial aircraft design process, with the objectives of enhancing safety and customer efficiency. Although this evolution was first initiated by an Airbus employee, it must be situated in the context of an epoch for aviation and human science. In 1996, the US authorities launched a worldwide review of HF integration in the aeronautical domain, where the FAA (Federal Aviation Administration) called on very well-known and legitimate HF scientists. Following statistical analyses of commercial accidents and incidents, human errors were identified, and continue to be identified, as a first-rate causal factor [4]. At the same time, it had become obvious that the human sciences could not only offer an explanatory assessment of aviation accidents but could also provide a positive contribution in aircraft design and operations. This resulted in the definition of a first lever for an efficient HOF approach: the role of regulators.

3 The Role of Regulators: Pushing Safety Requirements and HOF Induction

The first lever driving considerations of human factors in product certification was the "strong recommendation" from the FAA to use "at the edge human science knowledge". This shared awareness between industries, academics and regulators gradually led to an evolution of the certification texts. This initiative was part of a time of formalization and dissemination of human science knowledge in a way usable by the industry. Of course, a series of ergonomics criteria, automation and computerization considerations [3] already existed but spread across various documents [2]. The first ISO 13407 (Human centered design process for interactive systems) was issued in 1999 before being extended to ISO 9241 [6] which incorporated a huge number of relevant requirements and guidance to support a "User centered design" approach. Standards and regulations are today available to regulate new aircraft projects (ARP 5056 [1], CS 25-1302, RTCA SC-233). They define safety standards and set out strong recommendations for demonstrating compliance to regulations. Beyond the HF criteria, compliance also recommends setting up a HF process throughout the design and certification phases.

The regulators elaborate requirements on OF matters too. We cannot avoid mentioning a very important process that contributes to ensuring aviation safety: the SMS (Safety Management System). It is defined as: "*a systematic, explicit and comprehensive process for managing safety risks*". As a global risk management system, the Safety Management System provides for goal setting, planning, measuring performance and proposing action for improvement.

4 Standard HF Processes in Aircraft Design Engineering

Airbus fully defined and integrated its own "HF design & certification process" [8]. It is based on the adaptation of 9241-11 to Airbus context. Today it is considered to be a mature process for addressing the current human challenges. The Airbus Human Factors Design Process (HFDP) is a set of activities at system and aircraft level that defines (1) the human operators' tasks and needs; (2) the HF issues and benefits related to human(s)-machine interaction; (3) the expected performance of the human-machine; (4) the validation plan to demonstrate the expected performance of the human-machine. It can be done through analysis or simulation with end-users in the loop using a scenario-based approach; and finally demonstrating compliance with HF certification. The HF process application is led by HF specialists who work in an integrated team (end users, designers, HF) for the duration of a technical project.

Regulations do not only govern design, but also flight operations, procedures, pilot training, maintenance operations, simulator qualification in the form of the "Operational Suitability Data" (OSD) mandating that aircraft manufacturers, who have to submit data to EASA, consider important for safe operations.

As with the other Airbus processes, standardization is key and can be considered as a second lever towards long-term change in the industry.

The Airbus HFDP is part of the other engineering processes along with quality, safety, and validation processes. The Airbus design office numbers several thousands of engineers worldwide and even more when encompassing the extended enterprise perimeter. Standardized HF process, requirements and guidelines (such as a Cockpit Philosophy) and shared HF evaluation methods are contributing factors for developing a consistent cockpit and cabin product whatever the diversity of design teams or the diversity of profiles, culture, experiences and job assignment in the supply chain. Why is it so important to define a standard process? Because a repetitive process, independent from any specific context, is more likely to change the internal way of working. It allows a comprehensive application of the process without having to negotiate the conditions on a case by case basis.

Other industries developed or are currently developing their own HF process. In 2010, a group of industries coming from ground, air and naval transportation, powerplant and government bodies shared their best practices through a series of workshops under the AFIS umbrella [5]. AFIS stands for the French Association of System Engineering. Eurocontrol has also created a common HF process to steer Air Navigation Service Providers to develop and deploy the new Air Traffic Management solutions, for increasing traffic capacity in a consistent manner (Human Performance Assessment Process) as described in Pelchen-Medwed and Biede-Straussberger [7].

5 HOF: Governance and Organization

The third lever is HF governance. Engineering and customer services top management mandated in 2015 a HF board to ensure proper decision-making and follow up on HF activities. The HF board is a decision-making authority and is composed of top managers and high-level human factors experts. The top managers cover the functions for which human factors can highly impact aircraft safety, the health and safety of workers or the global efficiency of Airbus product for customers. Safety management needs a global consideration of human factors. It includes the definition of a clear, unified HOF strategy, policies and priorities for all Airbus products and processes (aircraft, documentation, training, maintenance, etc.). The board allows HOF to be considered as a cross-functional discipline across organizations. Aircraft safety, flight testing, systems design, industrial quality, aircraft programs, architecture and customer services are discussing how to establish a consistent philosophy on implementing and disseminating HOF throughout the aircraft cycle. For example, if an in-flight event that occurred in service is classified as human factors, it is analysed from the design and the operational point of view with a consistent model of human behavior. The HF board is key for assessing, explaining, analysing, and predicting the impact of HOF in political, economic and safety-related scenarios and decisions.

This decision board helps to promote the visibility and the legitimacy of human factors in the company. It reinforces the recognition and the authority of HF through the involvement of top managers. It is also a way to share and coordinate cross-organizations.

In term of implementing HF in the business, Airbus decided to organize HF in a decentralized manner. It means that several HF specialist teams are located near to their respective centres of competence. For instance, one HF organization is located in the cockpit design centre of competence, another one is in the cabin domain. High-level experts oversee technical coordination. A network of human factors specialists has been set up to allow any HF specialist to know and exchange with any HF colleague within Airbus overall.

On the production side, a similar network was organized as a real asset to cope with the specific difficulties of this sector. Unlike in the engineering environment, the ergonomics specialists are spread across the European plants and Final Assembly Lines (FAL) and can feel as if they are working in isolation from other HF specialists. Promoting networking inside a HF community is a favorable condition for HOF performance.

Poor ergonomics in manual handling operations are identified as the second most common cause of long-term injuries in the Airbus production sector. Musculo-Skeletal-Disorder (MSD) is the most common cause of absence with a significantly high number of days lost per year, as has been the case for many years. This awareness led to the implementation of a network of dedicated ergonomists working in all production plants across Europe.

The network is also covering the Final Assembly Lines (FAL). A central coordinator is in charge of managing the network, sharing best practices amongst the facilities and defining the strategy for ergonomics in production. One of the results is a common document of aligned rules, which are derived from international standards, national obligations and specific requirements in terms of ergonomics with respect to Health & Safety. They are applicable to all plants, FAL, and also provided when a new line design is subcontracted to suppliers. Based on the key indicator methods (holding, lifting, carrying, pulling, pushing) ergonomic conditions and MSD relevant activities are screened and anticipated.

Countermeasures are taken to correct the past and also prevent for the future.

Even when manual handling operations of loads and associated postures do not completely cover the full set of ergonomics, it is essential to interact at an early stage, referring to the known number of injuries.

Beside of these ergonomics considerations, workstation design on the shop floor is also influenced by different environmental factors i.e. organization (time), logistics (tasks and flows) and interaction (human-machine).

This becomes important whenever ergonomic analyses are made, especially when investigating alternative scenarios, working with collaborative robots, smart tools etc.

In order to get full integrity, we are aiming to achieve valuable ergonomic conditions across the chain of Engineering, Manufacturing and Maintenance.

This will reduce the number of lost time injuries and increase the safety and quality of work and ultimately the health of employees. Furthermore, it is key for future production design, helping the company to be competitive and efficient.

Quite recently and after a long period of "independence", the different HF organizations (engineering, customer services and production) moved closer in order to exchange on topics such as "human and robots", smart tools, cognitive assistants and the use of big data to better understand actual human operator behavior. The improved connection between Engineering and Manufacturing is not specific to HF, it is part of the 'factory of the future' project to better consider the manufacturability requirements in the design so as to reduce the lead time and cost of operations. HF should be involved at the appropriate level for the benefits of the workers and work organization.

One of our most important projects is now to collectively review the current HOF to face the future challenges as new concepts of operations (Reduced team operations, factory of the future, remote control room…) and new kind of technologies associated with increased automation, augmented intelligence systems, robots/cobots…Consequently, new HF competences, new ways of working and new standards need to be invented.

6 HOF Competence Management

The fourth lever is competence management. In-service event analysis shows that Runway Excursion, Loss of Control, and Control Flight Into Terrain are persistent events. Human error is often cited as a primary cause or contributing factor in most accidents. It means that we need to reinforce HF education in the aviation community: HF related to approach and landing management, energy management, attention allocation, crew fatigue, manual flying following automation degradation, or procedure management are just examples. As such, the competencies implemented to apply the HF approach are a combination of human sciences (cognitive psychology, linguistics, physiology, human-machine interaction, sociology), operational knowledge (pilots, cabin crew, etc.) and engineering skills. Airbus decided to recruit these specialists.

HF specialists are always a small group of people among thousands of engineers. They can be considered as "cost/time constraint" and of course as troublemakers when challenging the "expected human behaviors' assumptions" of the engineering staff. As a minority, human factors specialists should always demonstrate their added value in front of a "monocultural engineering world". Educating a large number of engineers and managers in HF should help to reinforce the efficiency of a multidisciplinary team, but it is costly. The aviation industry is helped by a series of initiatives that disseminate human science knowledge. For example, Yeh et al. [10] issued a report on human factors considerations in the design and evaluation of flight deck displays and controls. For its part, Airbus is currently developing a set of rich media and a knowledge pack using the company intranet and low-cost dissemination tools. Nevertheless, we are investing in HF experts and their career path. These experts are an asset for the company. They have a strong academic background in the most relevant human science disciplines and have acquired much on the job experience. They work together and are responsible for the development of HF competences in their centre of competences. They are known by the management and responsible for elaborating the vision in their domain of expertise.

But we can ask ourselves how to develop a stronger footprint, looking at how the "User eXperience (UX) design" community has rapidly won new markets. UX design is a process of designing (digital or physical) products that are useful, easy to use and, above all, a pleasure to interact with. It is about making sure the end users find a hedonic *value* in the usage of the product. Even if UX design studies have a direct impact on sale and revenue as they are directly impacting the "mass buyer" whereas HOF in industry is generally impacting the employee performance, and rather a source of cost and not a direct source of revenue. But let us be creative to offer the best product to the end users, integrating the conventional HF qualitative values and hedonic values in a same HF label.

7 Conclusion, HOF Maturity

Regardless of our efforts, these four levers cannot be enough to guarantee the success of the HOF approach in the future.

New technological developments and economic changes offer a large number of opportunities but also important challenges for organizations. Among these evolutions, autonomous transportation, connectivity, IOT (Internet Of Things), robotics and artificial intelligence will have a huge impact on human life as well as on human operators at work.

Staying aligned with the strategic objectives and preparing the future is paramount for companies. The previous levers for implementing HF standard processes, HF governance, and competence management are the critical ingredients of a HOF maturity framework to guarantee that:

- the projects deliver as expected,
- the projects selected are the ones that support the company strategy and bring the best benefits: selection of the most critical projects with a high added value. For example, the selection should include the "burning" projects, the ones that solve important issues in daily operations as well as the project that drive the research strategy,

- the teams have the appropriate knowledge, process, methods and tools,
- the HOF organization has the necessary capacity to continuously anticipate the evolutions (adaptability, change mindset),
- the HOF organization is sustainable and robust. It is independent enough from the human factors specialists in charge of HOF.

A suggestion would be to measure HOF maturity on a regular basis to identify and understand what is useful or not so useful, or to identify how to achieve a higher level of maturity.

This is key to setting up a valuable and sustainable HF approach.

The level of maturity should define the "predictability, effectiveness, and control of the HOF". HF governance allows the improvement process, that is the highest level of maturity. We could summarize the HOF maturity level in the Fig. 1.

The model provides a theoretical continuum along which process maturity can be developed incrementally from one level to the next. Skipping levels is not allowed/feasible.

As a conclusion, we may recommend setting up efficient HOF approaches. First of all, to integrate the HF processes into the current/existing business organizational model of the company processes, with the same level and the same visibility compared to other processes. Second, to set up HF governance at the higher level of management to share the risks of not having an appropriate HOF approach and define the suitable HF strategy. And third to elaborate relevant indicators to measure the maturity level of HOF and to monitor it on a regular basis to ensure optimal consideration of HOF. These fundamentals should allow us to shape the significant changes we see

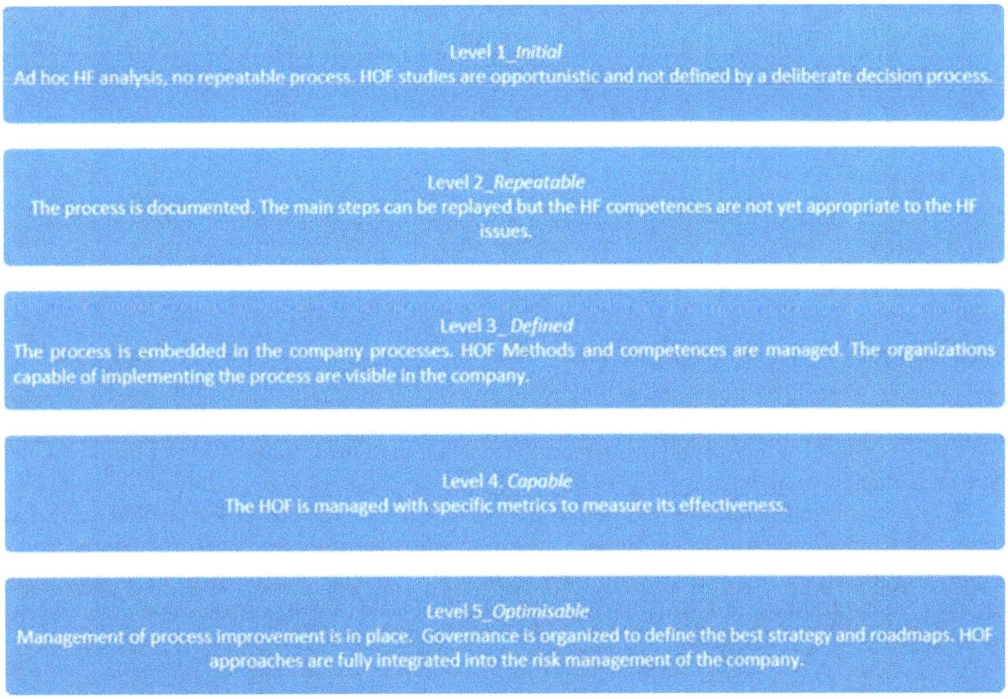

Fig. 1 Level of HOF maturity [adapted from integration of the test maturity model (TMMi [9])]

as robotics increase (between 1993 and 2007, robot density increased by more than 150%) or digitalization expands without overly penalizing the working conditions of human operators.

This is crucial for a business that must adapt to new market challenges and customer expectations.

References

1. ARP5056, Flight crew interface considerations in the flight deck design process for part 25 aircraft. SAE 2006-07-05 (n.d.), https://www.sae.org/standards/content/arp5056/
2. L. Bannon, Issues in design. Some notes, in *User-Centered System Design*, ed. by D.A. Normal, S.W. Draper (Lawrence Erlbaum Associates, 1986), pp. 25–29
3. C.W. Billings, in *Aviation Automation: The Search for a Human-Centered Approach* (Lawrence Erlbaum Associates, 1997)
4. FAA human factors team, The interfaces between flight crews and modern flight deck systems. FAA report (1996)
5. E. Gardinetti, D. Soler, F. Reuzeau, C. Maïs, X. Chalandon, Ingénierie des facteurs humains, in *ERGO IA2014*, Biarritz, October 2014
6. ISO 9241-210, Ergonomics of human-system interaction—Part 210: human-centred design for interactive systems (2010)
7. R. Pelchen-Medwed, S. Biede-Straussberger, Effectiveness of the application of the HP assessment process in SESAR1, in *USA/Europe ATM Seminar/Seattle*, 26–30 June 2017
8. F. Reuzeau, Human factors design process: benefits and success factors, in *3rd Human Dependability Workshop (HUDEP 2013)*, ESA. Munich, 13 & 14 November 2013
9. TMMi, Test maturity model integration, (the TMMi Model). TMMi Foundation (n.d.), https://www.tmmi.org/tmmi-model/
10. M. Yeh, J. Young, C. Donovan, S. Gabree, Human factors considerations in the design and evaluation of flight deck displays and controls. Version 1.0 final report—November 2013 DOT/FAA/TC-13/44 (2013)

Developing Human and Organizational Factors in a Company

Some Lessons from Ergonomics?

François Daniellou

Abstract The issue of the development of human and organizational factors of industrial safety in a company can be nourished by the experience gained from ergonomics. The author draws lessons from some French examples.

Keywords Ergonomics · Organizational design · Human factors

1 Introduction

"If we want to develop human and organizational factors in the company, how should we organize it?" This is basically the question that industrial groups have asked FonCSI to examine in this strategic analysis. The issue relates, of course, to the consideration of human and organizational factors *of industrial safety*. My past career as an ergonomics teacher leads me to suggest that it could usefully be nourished by an understanding of the successes and failures of the development of *ergonomics* in French companies.

The relationship between the terms *human and organizational factors* and *ergonomics* is unclear. For the International Ergonomics Association, *human factors* and *ergonomics* are simply synonyms, and are covered by the same definition:

> Ergonomics (or human factors) is the scientific discipline concerned with the understanding of interactions among humans and other elements of a system, and the profession that applies theory, principles, data and methods to design in order to optimize human well-being and overall system performance.

In the field of industrial safety, the terms *human factors* (HF) or *human and organizational factors* (HOF) have a wider scope: they refer to the multidisciplinary study of the conditions that foster an efficient and safe human activity, and they encompass the contribution of all individual and collective human sciences.

F. Daniellou (✉)
FonCSI, Toulouse, France
e-mail: francois.daniellou@foncsi.icsi-eu.org

B. Journé et al. (eds.), *Human and Organisational Factors*,
SpringerBriefs in Safety Management,
https://doi.org/10.1007/978-3-030-25639-5_6

The trend is towards a reconciliation of these two approaches: organizational dimensions are becoming more and more a concern for ergonomists, due to the development of interventions in design phases on the one hand, and to the prevention of musculoskeletal disorders and psychosocial risks on the other.

2 Some Industrial Examples

In France, the first industrial ergonomics lab was created in 1955 at Renault by Wisner [2]. While its founder wanted to address the ergonomics of plants as much as that of cars, the senior management did not permit it. Their main concern was to design cars that allowed the largest number of people to drive (and therefore buy) them. Only much later did ergonomists and "sociotechnical engineers" participate in the design of assembly lines: the concern was then to maintain in employment a large population of workers aged over 40.

In the field of chemistry, Rhône-Poulenc played a pioneering role in the 1980s with the design of control rooms. After difficulties encountered at the start of several industrial projects, Jacques Laplace (a Human Resource manager), Denis Regnaud (a socio-technician) and Michel Guy (an ergonomist) formalized a systematic participatory HOF approach to design projects, including the early assignment of future operational teams, and their association with the project in the frame of an "Operational Project Team" [1]. Regrettably, after several years of success, investments in France dried up and the approach was discontinued.

In the aircraft industry, at Aerospatiale, a double development took place: on the one hand, a strong contribution of ergonomists to the industrial design of assembly lines emerged in the late 1980s; on the other hand, there was a notable development in the human factors of cockpit design after the Mont Saint-Odile accident (due to regulatory pressures and thanks to several internal and external sponsors). Those two dynamics have been perpetuated and are currently converging (see Florence Reuzeau's chapter in this book).

Assistance Publique Hôpitaux de Paris,[1] in the late 1980s, made the presence of ergonomists in the design of new hospital units mandatory and created for this purpose a central ergonomics department, which has now disappeared.

At EDF[2] the "ergonomics/HF" concern developed in several departments: in the occupational medicine department around occupational health, in the Nuclear Production Directorate for the issue of nuclear safety, particularly in the Engineering department for the design and modification of control rooms and procedures—drawing the lessons from Three Mile Island accident—, in the R&D department for nuclear safety, as well as for the usability of software and home automation.

This list of examples is, of course, non-exhaustive but may help us to try and draw some generalisable lessons.

[1]Which manages all public hospitals in Paris.

[2]The historical French electricity operator.

3 Some Success Factors

The emergence of "ergonomics/HF" departments always results from a combination of:

- a major threat for the company (industrial accident, repeated failure of investment projects, number of occupational diseases, low product attractivity…);
- the sustained involvement of internal individuals, educated in ergonomics, and of industrial decision makers who have been convinced by significant examples;
- in the case of energy and aeronautics, the role of regulatory bodies who pay attention to this focus and impose minimum standards.

The following factors of success may be identified.

3.1 A Close Connection between Practitioners and Academics

The development of French-speaking ergonomics has been marked by a strong connection between academic institutions and practitioners, including within SELF, the *Société d'ergonomie de langue française*. On the one hand, academics made important efforts to offer continuous education programmes for practitioners, allowing them to update their knowledge according to research developments. On the other hand, and most importantly, some labs have developed 'research on practice', starting from researchers' field interventions as well as from sustained interactions with internal or consultant practitioners. These exchanges allowed a common analysis of successes and difficulties, and the discussion of 'models' of interventions on various topics (in investment design projects, for the prevention of musculoskeletal disorders or psychosocial risks, etc.). Most ergonomists who were 'pioneers' in their company belonged to such academic networks.

3.2 Leading by Example

The story of the development of ergonomics in an organization often starts like this. Well before ergonomics/HF have an acknowledged status in the company, one or several individuals of relatively low rank, and/or an external consultant play an outstanding role in using HF methods to overcome a problem which the organization had, until then, been unable to resolve. Some such examples attract the attention of high-level decision makers, who firstly issue multiple requests, then advocate for an institutionalization of the approach.

3.3 Organization around Key Processes

The most sustainable examples are those where the ergonomics/HF approach is structured around the company's key processes.

Let us take the example of the PSA group, which employ several dozen ergonomists. Some of them contribute to vehicle design (increasingly so, due to the digitalization of driving). Others are assigned to the design of assembly lines and plant units (giving feedback on the car design to ensure its manufacturability), others to production plants. The last two groups have the same management team and ergonomists switch from one to the other.

The key processes—"product design", "design of production means", "operation"—are the most common, but probably not the only ones. Ergonomics/HF are usually mobilized to ensure (together or separately) safe and easy use of the product, production quality and occupational health and safety. In some cases, the humans who are the targets of the action are customers or users, in some cases they are employees, sometimes both (the design of a car that be saleable and manufacturable).

Of course, those key processes will evolve, as will the respective weights of the stakeholders who embody them. Detecting these evolutions and adapting the response is a key element of a sustained contribution of ergonomics.

3.4 Combining Ready-Made and Haute Couture

The sponsors of the ergonomics/HF approach rapidly became aware that it was not possible to have an ergonomist standing behind each design engineer to ensure, as a minimum, compliance with anthropometric and perceptive standards. It was necessary to guarantee and assess the integration of basic ergonomic prescriptions from the very first drawings, without waiting for the project reviews which generate late, expensive and conflict-provoking modifications.

One of the first tools designed with this objective was the famous 'Renault grid', which allowed for an early scoring of work stations, and led to prohibiting those that entailed significant risks. Like other tools that have successfully followed this one, it presented the following features:

- good usability, requiring only a few hours of training;
- a transversal nature, which made it a boundary object between designers, production managers and HF specialists;
- a mandatory character, with the commitment not to produce work stations with extreme scores;
- periodic revision—albeit not too often—to integrate new risks and new knowledge.

While being heavily criticized by the most purist external ergonomists for its 'simplistic' nature, this tool played a considerable role in the integration of an ergonomic 'minimum' throughout the whole group. It also freed up ergonomists for tailor-made interventions where their skills were mobilized at a higher level. Haute couture becomes a de facto necessity for the design of an efficient and safe work organization.

Beyond the circulation of these historical standards, some companies today provide managers and project leaders with HF procedures and methods, e.g. for analysing adverse events, anticipating the socio-organizational consequences of a change, etc. These approaches are the object of training programmes and an accompaniment by HF specialists.

3.5 *Associating Health and Performance*

If interest in occupational health and safety is real in some companies, for human and/or financial reasons, it is seldom enough of a concern to ensure the allocation of the resources needed for the structuration of ergonomics/HF in the organization.

The demonstration of the contribution of human work to the organization's global performance is always necessary, if this approach is to be implemented. It can be based on different statements: quality improvement (decrease of defects and scrap), increased flexibility of production, improvement in the operation rate of machinery, reduction in absenteeism and employee turnover, winning demanding clients, prevention of major industrial risks.

3.6 *Micro and Organization Levels*

One of the main features of the ergonomics/HF approach is to constantly connect the "microscopic" understanding of activity in the workplace with organizational or strategic dimensions. Many ergonomists have in the last 20 years followed a route that led to influence higher order determinants, those connected to work and company organizations. This attempt proves more successful when their intervention occurs at the early stages of technical or organizational design rather than in curative actions.

3.7 *The Central/Decentralized Mix*

In many cases, the structuration of the ergonomics/HF approach combines:

- specialists who are seconded close to the operational trades and sites, whose actors and processes they know in depth;

- a light-handed central team, which defines generalisable processes and fosters the sharing and capitalization of experiences. They also act as a two-way relay with the top management.

This structure is similar to the one that can be found in HSE departments in many cases.

3.8 Some Specialists and a Network

Whatever their number and competence, ergonomists alone cannot detect and influence all processes where a HF approach would be required. They must rely on a dual network:

- an internal network of correspondents, interested managers and, in certain cases, personnel representatives, who have been trained and act as informants and relays with the trades;
- an external network of trusted consultants, to whom some of the interventions may be subcontracted, and with whom a joint elaboration of generalizable lessons is possible.

3.9 A Solid and Discreet Theory

In countries inspired by 'activity ergonomics', training in ergonomics emphasises the gap between prescribed work and real work, the constant adaptation of the worker's operating strategies to cope with the variability of the work situation and his/her own variability, the importance of the vitality of the work group, the physiological, cognitive and psychological strain related to various tasks, etc. The curricula also provide classic intervention methods that may be adapted to each specific situation. The theoretical background of the ergonomist's intervention is a solid one and is regularly discussed and updated in professional meetings.

Nonetheless, the ergonomists' professional success relies mostly on their capacity to speak their partners' language rather than that of their professors and on their ability to introduce the HF approach as naturally as possible in existing structures and processes.

This dialogue requires the sharing of some HOF knowledge and practice with counterparts, through training programmes which allow them to discover how this approach may enlighten some of the issues they have to deal with and enhance their own professional practice.

4 Avenues for Progress

Although, in some companies, the HOF approach seems solidly anchored, major difficulties relate to:

(1) the sustainability of actions which have been launched by confident managers, and may be under threat when they leave;
(2) the interface between the different departments in charge of the domain.

(1) To address this vulnerability, it is necessary to anchor practices that become inescapable in the organization as a consequence of their broad dissemination and their acknowledged contribution.
(2) Taking the human contribution into account in design and organizational decisions is a multifaceted issue: it includes product usability, attractivity and safety; operability of industrial facilities, ergonomics of work stations; organization of R&D programmes; operational excellence, lean production; industrial safety, occupational health and safety; incentive and sanction policies, company's attractiveness, skills and age management, induction programmes and career management; social dialogue, participation, profit-sharing; industrial subcontracting policy…

In a major group, these issues are supported by different departments, that may carry distinct models of the human and of the organization. These organizational silos may be a source of contradictions. A well-known hospital example is the contradiction between wearing gloves, which is prescribed by the occupational health department to protect caregivers, and washing hands, which is recommended by the patient safety department to prevent nosocomial infections.

Individual contact between specialists from these different worlds usually exists, of course. What is at stake today is a shared (and therefore debated) vision of the conditions of human work that is efficient, safe, favourable to personal development, and a deep understanding of its contribution to the company's global performance.

If the horizon of such a generalization may seem distant, two dynamics may contribute to bringing it closer:

- Serious HOF educational programmes for managers and personnel representatives (at the university level as well as in the company) that help to overcome such clichés as "if all procedures were followed, there would be no problem" or "what you can't measure doesn't exist", and make it possible to establish minimal HOF steps in the processes;
- Multiple interactions between Human Resources, engineering departments, production, HOF and health specialists, in a context of technical and organizational design projects implemented with the strong participation of operation managers, employees and personnel representatives.

What is eventually at stake is less the structuring of a HOF department than 'HOFizing the organization',[3] or in other words, impregnating it with concern for the conditions of efficient and safe human work.

References

1. J. Laplace, D. Regnaud, Démarche participative et investissement technique: la méthodologie de Rhône-Poulenc, in *Cahiers techniques UIMM*, vol. 52 (UIMM, Paris, 1986)
2. A. Wisner, *Quand voyagent les usines* (Syros, Paris, 1985)

[3]According to Hervé Laroche.

Organisational Factors, the Last Frontier?

Ivan Boissières

Abstract Significant advances have been made in the field of human and organisational factors (HOF) integration in industrial groups these last decades. Nowadays, HOF are generally quite structured in companies, in the form of a coalition between a few key departments and their allies. Nevertheless, various features limit their scope, notably in their impact on the organisation. First, we must acknowledge that the 'o' in Human and organisational Factors is a small 'o'. What lies behind this statement is that the human factors approach dominates, and the purely organisational approach is given far less attention. Then the various approaches usually remain limited to safety issues. HOF issues are rarely considered in strategic trade-offs, or in restructuring or management discussions. Finally, since the success of HOF implementation is mostly built on the political will and relationships of a few key individuals with top managers, they usually do not persist when these people leave. Beyond these observations, this chapter, based on a solid experience of HOF approaches that have been implemented since the 2000s in different industrial sectors, explores the underlying reasons for these limitations and proposes some ways forward for a better integration and sustainability of HOF in high-risk companies.

Keywords Organisational factors · HOF coalition · HOF supply

1 Introduction: Human and Organisational Factors with a Small "O" (HoF)

Many high-risk companies often present the incorporation of human and organisational factors (HOF) as the last step in their safety strategy, after having first taken essentially technical then procedural measures.

There is no doubt that this approach has allowed progress to be made in the dissemination of the major concepts illustrating the human contribution to safety. For example, there is a growing acceptance of the difference between work as done

I. Boissières (✉)
Icsi, Toulouse, France
e-mail: Ivan.Boissieres@icsi-eu.org

B. Journé et al. (eds.), *Human and Organisational Factors*,
SpringerBriefs in Safety Management,
https://doi.org/10.1007/978-3-030-25639-5_7

and work as imagined. Many companies are considering the importance of managed safety as a complement to rule-based safety and this tends to be reflected in their structuring of human and organisational factors.

However, some practices are struggling to truly evolve:

- Major reorganisations are still essentially technocratic and their impact on work groups and safety is rarely anticipated.
- Beyond awareness campaigns with little or no follow-up, it is very difficult to invest in HOF skills for operational managers.
- Leadership from company executives is affected by a high turn-over rate, thus undermining continuity in terms of HOF approaches.
- Safety is still only marginally integrated into the organisation's key processes (design, human resources, finances, etc.). Therefore, its place in the strategic decision-making process can be seriously weakened when the company is experiencing financial turbulence.

On closer examination, these limitations seem to be concentrated around organisational factors in the broad sense. Could it be that the term HOF actually hides different realities? It must be acknowledged that the 'o' in human and organisational factors often is a small 'o'. On the one hand there is the progress made by the human factors approach, which focuses closely on workers and the reality in the field. On the other hand, it seems to be more difficult to change the organisation and managerial practices.

We propose to examine this hypothesis in more depth, based on experience of HOF approaches implemented since the 2000s in high-risk companies.[1] We will more specifically explore potential causes of this blockage not on the demand side (resistance of organisations to change their practices), but rather on the HOF supply side. Are the experts' profiles relevant? Are there difficulties in appropriating fields mostly peopled by general consultants and gurus and considered to be scientifically weak? Is the HOF "coalition" powerful enough to allow an actual consideration of HOF in companies?

2 Is the Role of Organisational Factors in the HOF Domain Actually a Problem of Supply?

One of the main reasons why it is so difficult to fully take organisational issues into account might be the profile of HOF suppliers, who are nearly all psychologists and ergonomists, to the detriment of sociologists and management scientists. We truly owe a lot to this community for raising the profile of human factors in companies.

[1] This chapter is above all based on a personal experience of consideration of HOF in companies: first as a Ph.D. fellow, then as an operational manager in a foreign subsidiary, and as an internal or external adviser to the executive management of large French groups, in various sectors: telecommunications, energy, transports, construction… Therefore, it may not be exempt from some overgeneralizations or caricatures.

However, consideration of organisational factors seems to be limited by some of their specificities such as the areas they choose to work in, their relationship to management, or even the theoretical framework.

The domains where human factors are considered relevant have changed greatly. The focus has moved from operator protection, to optimizing their work, safety and performance. There seems to be a desire to slowly 'climb' from the micro (the work situation) to more macro dimensions related to the organisation of work. This has been most successful in the field of the design (of a workstation or a factory). But it has very rarely been used to address large-scale managerial or organisational change.

An organisational intervention also means changing who HOF specialists talk to. Historically, they have been invited in by departments that are doing quite similar work, such as the medical service or internal ergonomists. They also have interacted a lot with front-line managers, i.e. the production or design team at the factory or project level. Working on the organisation and major strategic decisions involves a shift from the production line to the management line, or even to the level of general management [2]. This represents a jump that is often difficult for HOF specialists to make because they do not want to lose their credibility with workers in the field or to be manipulated due to lack of leeway.

Finally, organisational factors appear to be a domain that is reserved for another category of stakeholders—auditors and management consultants. The business world is, in some ways, implicitly divided in two. Human factors approaches apply to working conditions (workers, safety, design) while auditors or management consultants work on organisational problems, management and strategic decisions. It is apparently difficult to overcome this division because, on the one hand, the human factors community is very critical of the lack of scientific knowledge of management consultants and of some so-called gurus. On the other hand, not many of these experts are interested in safety issues. There do not seem to be many bridges between the two worlds, especially since organisational sociologists—whose work is closer to the ideas of human and organisational factors—have almost disappeared from companies. In the nineties, it was common to find sociologists working at the top level in companies such as Air France, RATP, Danone, Michelin, etc. As an example, during my PhD at France Telecom, I worked with a sociologist who advised the general management to support the reorganisation of one of its departments [4]. Nowadays, the demand from companies for sociological support is so low, it is hardly possible to quote such an example [6, 8]. The lack of development of organisational aspects in HOF approaches is harmful because it risks locking those approaches into an overly-limited view of the problem. Above all, rather like a 'glass ceiling', it might block access to the level where solutions can most often be found: organisational, management or strategic decisions.

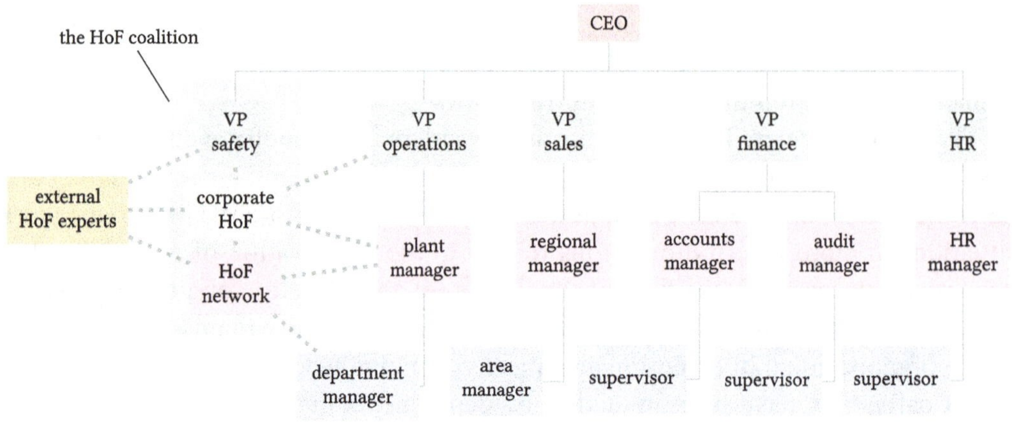

Fig. 1 The HOF 'coalition': the current situation

3 The Current HOF "Coalition"

How is the HOF approach currently structured in at-risk companies in France? Who are the key actors, the members of the coalition that is driving progress? Where are they located in the organisation?

First, we will address the external options the French HOF market has to offer. As already stated in this chapter, the supply is mostly composed of experts with experience in human factors and ergonomics, working in small consulting companies. This community is well-structured; its members are part of an association, the SELF (The Society of French-speaking Ergonomists) and they regularly meet to share their experience. In fact, there are many more of these external consultants than internal experts.

Secondly, what are the current trends within companies? Based on experience with several large industrial groups, some conclusions can be drawn (Fig. 1).

Some at-risk companies have centralised their HOF expertise. It may be the responsibility of a single person, usually a former consultant, or an HSE[2] employee who has specialized in human and organisational factors. At best, it is a department combining these profiles. In any case, it is a very lightweight structure that aims to promote HOF approaches or to capitalize on local experiments in order to disseminate them. It can also be supported by an R&D department staffed by HOF researchers.

In some leading companies, there might be HOF specialists posted in the field. In some cases, they have organised themselves into a network. For example, at the French national railway company (SNCF[3]) or in the nuclear sector, there are human factors consultants. But the relationship between headquarters and this decentralised network is not always easy. On-site experts work closely with their colleagues and

[2]Health, Safety and Environment.

[3]*Société nationale des chemins de fer français.*

have more in common with local managers than with a centralised HOF unit. Sometimes, they do not even belong to the same sector. At SNCF, for instance, the human factors network is part of the human resources department and mainly deals with the quality of life at work and occupational safety. Meanwhile, in the same company, the central HOF department is part of the industrial safety division!

In the vast majority of cases, HOF falls within the remit of HSE structures, or those responsible for major risks. For example, at Air France, the HOF unit is part of flight safety. At SNCF it is part of railway safety, and at EDF,[4] a French electric utility company, of nuclear safety.

Finally, this small internal network, which is often somewhat disconnected, takes its orders from a few decision makers who are convinced that the HOF approach can help them solve their operational problems. However, these managers are still very much in the minority, which generally leads to ad hoc requests. The Institute for an industrial safety culture (Icsi), created in 2003 following the AZF accident in Toulouse (France), promotes a collective dynamic which allowed to launch large safety culture reinforcement programmes based on better consideration of HOF. However, although these approaches are often initiated by top managers, they appear difficult to maintain in the long-term when these managers change positions or leave the company.

4 Proposals for Ways Forward

To overcome some of the limitations described above and reinforce the HOF coalition so that it can work on organisational issues, here are a few ideas based on our experience working with industrial companies.

4.1 Managers/Senior Executive Staff: Reaching a Critical Mass

The first suggestion regards the relationship between HOFs and top managers. Connecting these two "worlds" is not easy because many top managers just have a few vague ideas about HOF or have developed their own way of doing things. Typically, they see the organisation as a structure only, or a set of rules and procedures where top-down management and little participation from the employees prevail. They do not really consider the impact on teams or power struggles as they implement changes in the organisation.

This is exactly why HOF experts need to talk to the top managers. At the very least, this reconciliation would allow them to share the basis of a common vision and overcome some stereotypes. This should help to avoid misunderstandings or failures.

[4]*Electricité de France.*

Thus, the challenge is to build a critical mass of top managers who are open to the HOF approach, rather than have a few lonely evangelists within the organisation. Moreover, it is of importance that HOFs do not remain enclosed within the safety department, because there is a risk of disconnection from the organisation's other strategic challenges.

4.1.1 Training: HOF as a Dimension of Management and not as a Standalone Topic

Training plays a key role in the integration of HOF in companies, and there are certain conditions that might foster success. In France, at least two training programmes had a significant impact on HOF in the industry.

Icsi
In 2005, Icsi and François Daniellou launched a 2-day training programme on HOF. This has proved successful since over 300 professionals attended it, creating demand for an executive master in HOF in partnership with ESCP Europe Business School. To date, more than 150 managers have studied for this master's degree (https://www.escpeurope.eu/programmes/executive-masters/executive-mastere-specialise-manager-des-organisations-a-risques). Unfortunately, participants mainly consisted of HSE specialists and very few were senior managers or Executive Committee members.

CEDEP[5]
Another training programme delivered by CEDEP is specifically targeted at Executive Committee members of Sanofi and L'Oréal. This programme is very successful and HSE specialists are not the majority of participants. However, it does not meet HOF standards. The training session starts with leadership, organisational culture and change management, and safety is addressed only much later.

These examples illustrate how difficult it is to get operational managers to attend HOF training. It also shows that a promising avenue is to integrate HOF into managerial training programmes instead of asking managers to attend specific HOF sessions. Moreover, one of the conclusions of the strategic analysis carried out by FonCSI[6] on professionalism is that safety should be better integrated into professional development rather than being taught separately [3, 7].

The best way to reach top management is with specially designed, internal training programmes.

[5]The Executive Education department of the INSEAD business school (European Institute of Business Administration).

[6]Foundation for an industrial safety culture.

"HSE for Senior Executives" and "HSE for Managers", Total
From 2011, Total launched 2–4-day training programmes targeting senior top executives and managers, respectively. The whole top management stratus is required to follow this course that is based on a 360-degree assessment of safety leadership and solid face-to-face training in HOF, followed by regular coaching.

Vinci Construction
More recently, Vinci Construction developed a one-and-a-half-day internal training programme called "Managing Through Safety", with a significant focus on HOF. It is part of "Cap for Management", the general, 6-day training programme for Vinci managers. It covers the fundamentals of management: finance, HR, business, innovation, etc. Even though the top executives stay for just a day and a half, the part they attend is dedicated to safety.

4.1.2 …so that Managers' Vision and Practices Can Evolve

The integration of HOF to other managerial challenges implies that current HOF specialists should be receptive to general management topics like power relations, corporate culture, leadership, change management, etc. It also involves encouraging more leadership or change management specialists to take an interest in safety. And, finally, it means that the topic should be included in internal management training courses, and externally by getting business schools to offer HOF training.

The real challenge is not to improve the marketing of HOF training programmes for managers. Above all, the objective is to profoundly change the attitudes of managers and management models that often represent an obstacle to giving proper consideration to HOF in companies.

4.1.3 Open up HOF Networks to Operational Managers

We stated earlier that decentralized HOF networks are sometimes found in companies with on-site internal consultants, or in business divisions. But they are usually made up of HOF specialists with a background in ergonomics and they find it difficult to influence important decisions since managers do not recognize their operational competence. Attracting more operational managers to HOF courses strengthens HOF networks by benefiting from their business profile.

EDF
At EDF, human factor consultants working in nuclear plants now operate in pairs made up of an external human factors expert or ergonomist, and someone else with operational experience and solid training in HOF.

SNCF Traction
Each year, 2–3 executives from SNCF traction, the train driver division, complete the Icsi executive master's degree in HOF. Over time, this has created an internal HOF network of operational staff. Today, SNCF Traction is one of the places where most progress has been made in HOF—both at the SNCF level and at the level of French industry. This was made possible thanks to a director who is a leader in the domain, and the network that played a determining role in driving the deployment of HOF initiatives internally.

4.2 *Strengthen Alliances with Other Actors*

Safety is not the only risk that businesses must manage. Production is fundamental too—and HOF specialists have a long history of talking to engineering firms about the technical details of projects in order to anticipate operational risks. Furthermore, a poor social climate and financial problems are other major risks that threaten the company's survival. If HOF is going to play a role in the company's trade-offs, it must be better integrated into the other departments concerned.

4.2.1 Human Resources Department

An alliance with the human resources department seems easiest, probably because this is where there are most bridges with safety and HOF.

Psychosocial risk issues are now being closely monitored by human resources departments, often with the support of experts. It is now accepted that the root causes of psychosocial risks are embedded in the organisation and management. Adopting this angle of attack would not only mobilize human and organisational factors but would do it by means of a topic linked to the organisation.

Some other issues interface easily with human resources, one of which is training. We already highlighted the importance of managers training in HOF. Indeed, it helps to get closer to human resources departments and allows a collaborative work on the evolution of the management model that will serve as a basis for internal or external training.

Another example of topics at the interface with human and organisational factors is "just culture". When translated at the level of an organisation, "just culture" is about drawing up clear and fair policies in terms of recognition of good practices/sanction of bad practices. Typically, it falls within the domain of human resources, but it is also very fashionable in the safety world at the moment [5].

4.2.2 Audit Departments

When it comes to investment decisions, any alliances must eventually extend to other influential departments such as compliance and audit departments. This process is just starting. As an example, a renowned human factors expert recently took part in an audit and regulatory review [1]. Conversely, for the first time a financial controller attended the Icsi HOF executive master in 2018.

4.2.3 Trade Unions/Regulatory Authorities

In addition to the managerial chain of command and internal managers, two other institutional actors, union and staff representatives and regulatory authorities may be effective partners.

Providing union representatives with HOF training represents a valuable investment because it creates internal pressure for organisational factors to be considered at a very high level. A major French trade union, CFDT, and more specifically its chemical energy federation, has created a major risks network and have taken HOF to heart. They trained themselves and drew up internal policies on safety topics which have been distributed to staff committees on all sites. Their influence has led to real progress.

Exxon Mobil—CFDT

CFDT representatives at a large Exxon Mobil site asked for a safety culture survey to be carried out. The analysis of this assessment led to the creation of a working group that brought together directors, the local chemistry federation, regional officials, union representatives, regulatory authorities, etc. It is not common to have such diverse actors at the same table. It generated a discussion of great interest, at a very high level, about how each organisation could help to improve industrial safety based on HOFs.

Finally, regulatory authorities are another solid ally that can, if needed, put more-or-less friendly pressure on company managers to consider HOF. The influence of international authorities in aeronautics is addressed in this book (see Florence Reuzeau's chapter, this volume). In the nuclear sector, the authority is carrying out fundamental work into human and organisational factors on various topics including industrial policy and subcontracting. There has not been any strong commitment so far, but it has, at least, forced the various stakeholders in the French nuclear sector to ask questions and eventually to agree on the way forward.

5 Concluding Remarks: Use Short-Term Wins to Sustain Long-Term Progress

It must be recognized, of course, that the different propositions discussed in this chapter are difficult to implement. Therefore, it is of paramount importance to establish a strategy for implementing HOF over a longer timeframe. Like any project that seeks to implement change, a two-step approach is needed: quick wins and long-term structured action.

5.1 In the Short Term: HOF Quick Wins

Before going any further, HOF must be put on the agenda and win in the short term. Here follow a few examples of quick win initiatives. A conference or a training session for directors conducted by an excellent speaker, is an efficient way of stimulating interest in going further. Similarly, videos or e-learning courses are good ways to introduce the topic.

> **E-learning**
> Icsi recently developed a short, e-learning module intended for directors and managers of a large industrial group to raise awareness about HOF. This was rapidly followed by further training for prevention specialists and managers at a local site, and a request from the CEO for a HOF study.

A safety culture assessment is another good way to open the door to more advanced HOF approaches—notably as it speaks to managers who love indicators. The starting point is safety issues, but it can go on to highlight organisational causes, such as managerial leadership, or reward and sanction policies. The most important aspect is that the clients should be management committees and not limited to safety managers.

These approaches are sometimes criticized by purists on the pretext that they are not ambitious enough, or that they tell the client only what they want to hear. However, considering them as a first step, they can be an effective way to get a foot in the door. Once you have done that, HOF approaches can be developed and implemented over time.

5.2 Anchoring HOFs in Companies: Key Actions

The actual issue at stake is to institutionalize HOF approaches in companies, especially in terms of organisational and strategic processes. Companies should seize opportunities related to specific moments of their life: some steps can be particularly conducive to launching a HOF approach. One interesting example is to integrate safety and HOF issues when the company is planning a major restructuring. Another opportunity is the implementation of a policy of formalizing the skills managers are expected to have. As an example, Suez has drawn up a guide for managers where principles like "the right to make mistakes" and the need to recognize the contribution of workers are made clear.

In a nutshell, integration and sustainability of HOF approaches in high-risk companies mostly rely on going beyond the glass ceiling by reaching a critical mass of executives open to HOF concepts, reinforcing alliances with other key sectors such as human resources, unions and regulatory bodies, and capitalizing on quick wins to sustain long-term progress.

References

1. R. Amalberti, La sécurité industrielle est-elle un art du compromis? Audit, risques et contrôle (12), 25–28 (2017), https://www.foncsi.org/fr/blog/article-a-r-c-rene-amalberti
2. R. Amalberti, F. Mosneron-Dupin, *Facteurs humains et fiabilité: quelles démarches pratiques* (Octares, Toulouse, 1997)
3. C. Bieder, C. Gilbert, B. Journé, H. Laroche, *Beyond Safety Training: Embedding Safety in Professionnals Skills* (Springer, 2017). https://doi.org/10.1007/978-3-319-65527-7
4. I. Boissières, *Une approche sociologique de la robustesse organisationnelle: le cas du travail des réparateurs sur un grand réseau de télécommunication.* Doctoral dissertation, Université de Toulouse 2, Toulouse (2005)
5. S. Dekker, *Just Culture: Balancing Safety and Accountability* (Ashgate, 2012)
6. F. Dupuy, *La Faillite de la pensée managériale. Lost in Management*, vol. 2 (Seuil, Paris, 2015)
7. FonCSI, *La sécurité, une affaire de professionnels ? Intégrer la sécurité aux compétences professionnelles.* Fondation pour une culture de sécurité industrielle (Foncsi, Toulouse, France, 2018), https://www.foncsi.org/fr/publications/collections/cahiers-securite-industrielle/securite-affaire-professionnels
8. La sociologie sur commandes?, Sociologies pratiques (36) (2018)

Risk Management and Judicialization

Caroline Lacroix

Abstract Industrial or public transport accidents are referred to the court of justice and often result in high-profile trials. This criminalization process raises the question of the place of repressive justice and the issue of the debate around the judicialization of such serious events. Beyond that, how is this penalization translated? Since the actual conditions for the safety of at-risk activities rely on a set of factors (compliance with norms, rules and procedures, experience of safety culture actors, etc.), how does the judge assess fault and what place is allocated to expertise?

Keywords Judicialization · Disaster · Risks · Criminal trial · Involuntary manslaughter · Responsibilities · Judge · Expertise

1 Introduction

Public transport, industrial and high-tech activities are likely to generate risks. Disasters always lead to the same questions: why and how did it occur? Could the damage have been avoided? What was done by those whose mission is to ensure the safety of all? The criminal justice system often appropriates these questions in order to seek answers, in a phenomenon known as judicialization or penalization. Judicialization of risky activities recently featured in the news in France when, on October 31th, 2017, the Paris Court of Appeal convicted the Grande Paroisse company and its director over the AZF disaster.

C. Lacroix (✉)
Université d'Evry-Val d'Essonne – Paris-Saclay, Évry, France
e-mail: caroline.lacroix@univ-evry.fr

B. Journé et al. (eds.), *Human and Organisational Factors*,
SpringerBriefs in Safety Management,
https://doi.org/10.1007/978-3-030-25639-5_8

2 Judicialization and Penalization

The term judicialization appeared in political discourse in the 1990s. It can thus be understood as the expanding role of judges in monitoring compliance by certain companies. The notion of "criminal justice" more specifically refers to "criminalization" or penalization after an accident. It is understood, first, as the recourse to criminal justice, either through the work of the public prosecutor's office or on the initiative of victims or associations. Penalization can also express "the reinforcement of penal repression", emphasizing either the propensity to question particular categories of hitherto protected citizens (local elected officials or business leaders) or to apply criminal law to activities that had been spared it in the past. The notion of penalization is then often used in a pejorative way and accompanied by a qualifier reinforcing this idea, such as that of "outrageous criminalization".

2.1 A Global Phenomenon?

Intervention by the criminal justice system is an integral part of the social response to a disaster. Disasters have entered the criminal field and this phenomenon is neither recent, nor uniquely French. A simple retrospective look at the legislation and practices of member countries of the European Union shows that most major transport or industrial accidents are played out on the criminal stage in all their variations and facets [10]. We mainly studied our close European neighbours: Germany, Spain, Italy, Belgium, Luxembourg and Great Britain. But beyond these few examples, we observed that other European countries do not exclude the use of criminal law in the treatment of disasters. This was the case in Switzerland following the Überlingen Air Collision that killed 71 people on July 1, 2002. A criminal trial was also held in Austria in connection with the Kaprun funicular accidental fire that caused 155 deaths on November 11, 2000. Each of these states has an administrative authority in charge of investigating the causes of the accidents. The administrative inquiry does not exclude the separate existence of a judicial inquiry and the holding of a criminal trial.

Contrary to popular belief, British disaster treatment is not limited to the issue of damage repair. The United Kingdom, often cited as a counter-example of the French criminalization movement, nevertheless tends to turn to criminal justice under the pressure of victims' lobbies. "*Disaster Action*", was founded as a charity in 1991 by survivors of disasters and bereaved people from the UK and overseas. They submitted to the Royal Commission on Criminal Justice a call for radical changes in the criminal justice system regarding the treatment of possible corporate crimes of violence. Thus, on April 6, 2008, the *Corporate Manslaughter and Corporate Homicide Act* was promulgated [1, 11, 12]. The creation of this new offence of manslaughter committed by a corporation provided a means of accountability for very serious management failings across an organisation. It is intended to work in conjunction with other forms of accountability such as gross negligence manslaughter for individuals and other elements of health and safety legislation.

2.2 *Why this Judicialization?*

There are several reasons for the attractiveness of criminal justice. Beyond procedural reasons, there are sociological explanations. Criminalization of disasters and referral to the criminal courts reflect both the social perception of risks and the social representation of criminal justice.

In the first place, the spirit of resignation is disappearing from our modern societies. As serious accidents multiply, disasters are no longer considered fate only, but also the result of risky human activities [2]. In one way or another, human activities may have triggered the disaster, or it may have been caused by a lack of forecasting, prevention or by inadequate safety management upstream. Meanwhile, the need for safety has become fundamental. The current trend is towards an almost absolute rejection of the inevitability of risks and the utopian affirmation of zero risk has been erected as a principle. This increased need for protection, even precaution, has found a resonance in law. Criminal law has a pronounced symbolic character. Our fellow citizens firmly believe that justice is not really done until those responsible have been given a criminal sentence.

Disasters therefore give rise to a process of dramatization of responsibilities. The criminal judge is perceived as "the only impartial interlocutor" [13], especially when the feeling of a "smothering of responsibilities" arises. Public opinion and victims share the same wish to acknowledge mistakes and identify their authors. Establishing the truth of the case is, as such, a remedy for the victim. The holding of a trial is useful not only to the victims but also to society. It constitutes a place for confrontation and dialogue, where searching for the veracity of the facts takes precedence even over the strict application of the law.

2.3 *The Protest*

This criminalization of major disasters is not unopposed. There is no shortage of arguments, both to justify the shortcomings of criminal law and to suggest other ways of managing collective accidents and/or "punishments" that are less egregious than the penal sanction. Some claim there should be sectoral criminal immunity or a reinforced presumption of innocence in highly technical fields. It is also argued that the fear of the criminal court results in a strict respecting of procedures, thus limiting innovation and ultimately undermining safety.

2.3.1 "Just Culture" and "Blame Culture"

> "Just Culture" is a culture in which front-line operators and others are not punished for actions, omissions or decisions taken by them which are commensurate with their experience and training, but where gross negligence, wilful violations and destructive acts are not tolerated. [8]

Successful implementation of safety regulations results in a "just culture" reporting environment within aviation organisations, regulators and investigation authorities. This is because one element of the philosophy of "just culture" is giving the actors sufficient leeway to allow them to share their mistakes during safety investigations without the risk of being systematically prosecuted in criminal cases.

By contrast, a "blame culture" is a description given to an organisation in which people are blamed for mistakes.

In this sense, the intervention of the criminal justice system in the context of disasters would thus be an example of blame culture, unlike the philosophy of "just culture". Indeed, penalization of disasters would precisely lead to the refusal of witnesses to co-operate in investigations, invoking their right to protect themselves from criminal prosecution. This would cause a breakdown in the feedback experience. Thus, penalization would harm safety.

2.3.2 The Case of Civil Aviation

The protest movement against penalization is particularly prevalent in civil aviation. In 2006, the Civil Air Navigation Services Organisation (CANSO), the Royal Aeronautical Society in England (RAeS) and the French National Academy of Air and Space (ANAE), adopted a resolution on the penalization of aviation accidents in which the signatory organisations stated that they

> (…) are convinced that criminal investigations and prosecutions in the wake of aviation accidents can interfere with the efficient and effective investigation of accidents and prevent the timely and accurate determination of probable cause and issuance of recommendations to prevent recurrence (…) [7].

According to these professionals, most aviation accidents result from human errors, often multiple and inadvertently committed. They declared that, in the absence of

> acts of sabotage and willful or particularly egregious reckless misconduct (including misuse of alcohol or substance abuse), criminalization of aviation accidents is not an effective deterrent or in the public interest. […] Increasing safety in the aviation industry is a greater benefit to society than seeking criminal punishment for those "guilty" of human error or tragic mistakes [7].

Such an approach found favour with the European Economic and Social Committee (EESC). In an opinion on the "Proposal for a regulation of the European Parliament and of the Council on the investigation and prevention of accidents and incidents in civil aviation", this body

> stresses the utmost importance for aviation safety of a truly independent accident investigation process free from interference from the affected parties as well as from the public, politics, media and judicial authorities. (...) EESC welcomes "Charter for just culture" agreed by the European civil aviation social partners on 31 March 2009 [4].

Thus, the European Union seems receptive to the principle of just culture. The term "just culture" is mentioned in the opening remarks of the 2010 regulation, as paragraph 24 states:

> The civil aviation system should equally promote a non-punitive environment facilitating the spontaneous reporting of occurrences and thereby advancing the principle of 'just culture' [5].

As an extension of the European Charter for a Just Culture adopted by the social partners of the European civil aviation sector on 31 March 2009.

But European Union law does not promote any kind of diversion. Indeed, the assertion of the need to separate the judicial inquiry from the administrative one in the European regulations does not, in any way, compel the abandonment of the judicial inquiry or establish a hierarchy between these investigations. No primacy of the administrative inquiry is affirmed. It is at best a recommendation, without binding legal effect for the Member States.

In fact, opposing just culture and penalization is the result of a pernicious amalgam. Just culture and a criminal trial do not occur at the same time and place. Just culture seeks to continuously improve safety and not identify individual responsibilities. Although it thus promotes a non-punitive atmosphere, just culture is not a system of total impunity. Rather, it is a proactive system intended to anticipate accidents by creating a climate of confidence favourizing the identification of any type of information relevant for safety. However, just culture does not mean there cannot be prosecutions when an accident occurs, notably if it has dramatic consequences.

3 The Expression of the Penalty

3.1 Foundation of Repression

The charge of unintentional crimes is used to ensure punishment via the courts of those at the origins of catastrophes. Most disasters are caused by the offences of manslaughter or accidental injury occurring as a result of negligence, carelessness, inattention or the accidental destruction, damage deterioration of property through an explosion or fire.

These terms all refer to imprudence, negligence, breaches of regulation, whose degree of seriousness is expressed as an ordinary fault (simple negligence), characterized fault (gross negligence i.e. fault exposing others to a serious danger its author could not ignore), deliberate fault (willful misconduct i.e. breach of duty of care or prudence).

Repression of imprudence, negligence liability, is a sensitive topic that has undergone two modifications since the entering into force of the Penal Code in 1994: first by the law of May 13th, 1996, then by the law of July 10th, 2000. These offences proceed from the following logic today: the degree of gravity of the fault constituting the offence is a function of the direct or indirect character of the causal link between this fault and the damage. When the causal link is direct, simple negligence is enough to engage the criminal responsibility of a natural person. When the causal link is indirect, the criminal responsibility of a natural person is engaged only in the case of willful misconduct or of gross negligence. To put it another way,

> The criminal responsibility of a natural person requires a gravity of the fault inversely proportional to the proximity of its harmful consequences [3].

The assessment of the fault must refer to the safety due diligence relative to the circumstances and characteristics of the agent. The law of 13 May 1996 strongly urged the criminal court to take into account the situation of the perpetrator. The legislator then provides the judge with the elements on which the assessment must be based: nature of the mission or functions, powers and means of the perpetrator. These criteria invite the judge to decide on objective data. It is a question of identification, in the conduct of the missions or the functions performed, in the exercise of the attributed competences, as well as in the use of the devolved powers and means, all the elements of a normal diligence. In criminal law, error is not considered a criminal fault. Not all errors are faults. The judge is not guided by a dogmatic but by a concrete approach, and is keen to consider the system of constraints under which safety actors work.

The objective of the law of 10 July 2000 was to tighten the hypotheses of liability of natural persons, indirect perpetrators, in matters of recklessness, by means of a linkage between the causal relation and the nature of the fault. This law tends to displace the repression towards the direct authors and the legal persons who in any event, remain responsible for all forms of imprudence, however slight.

3.2 *Typology of Responsibilities*

Accidents and disasters are often caused by a combination of factors: degree of compliance with norms, rules and procedures, behaviour of safety actors. The industrial safety policy is analysed by the criminal judge, who will highlight the absence, the inefficient implementation of this policy. The judge is also interested in human and organisational factors in high-risk companies. By seeking the implication of human factors, not only can compensation be obtained but also the reparation of any damage. This power of repair of justice is most embodied in the criminal trial [9].

Today, there is a real "disasters" case law framework. The essential respect for safety in high-risk organisations is recalled through the judgments rendered. Analysis of the various court decisions makes it possible to draw up both a typology of the behaviours that can lead to convictions and the profile of potentially responsible persons in case of a disaster. The chain of causalities extends from mere agents to decision makers. Court decisions include the whole decision-making and safety hierarchies of the company. These malfunctions in terms of safety can also be attributed to the legal person. In the end, these court decisions also make it possible to build HOF approaches to industrial safety in a large group.

3.2.1 Natural Person

In the search for multiple responsibilities, there is a real methodology implemented by magistrates that is reflected in the form of the decisions rendered, which present an originality in the way they are written. The most obvious manifestation of this modus operandi appears in the ranking of potential authors, through a process of " grouping by responsibility".

A first group consists of the company managers and executives. These are the persons for whom the works are carried out and who have an economic interest in the activity at the origin of the harmful event. Imprudence or negligence committed at the highest hierarchical level of the company is therefore sanctioned. Then there is a second group, those who could be called the "men of art", the entrepreneurs and architects. They are potentially responsible since they are the ones who build and create. Another group of officials is sometimes made up of what might be called "safety officers". Ultimately there is the person directly responsible for the disaster, the one that we could call "the lamplighter". This first link in the causal chain is often an artisan or a worker. However, the faults committed by these immediate perpetrators are often only evidence of much more serious mistakes committed upstream, some of which can be blamed on public actors.

3.2.2 Legal Person

Disasters often have structural causes and the lack of safety at the origin of the drama is sometimes the result of an explicit corporate policy. Through the implementation of the liability of legal persons, the judge can adequately sanction the organisational factors of a company. These safety dysfunctions can be attributed to the legal person since the entering into force of the Penal Code in 1994, a major innovation.

The liability of a legal person may coexist with that of natural persons. It can be engaged for a simple fault of recklessness whatever the nature of the causal link. The decriminalization resulting from the reform of 10 July 2000 seeking to distinguish between direct and indirect causality, has been established only for the benefit of natural persons. Thus, the purpose is to compensate the decriminalization of natural persons by the responsibility of legal persons.

4 The Judge and Expert Opinions

As stated earlier in this chapter, in France, an industrial disaster usually leads to two different investigations, pursuing different objectives: an administrative inquiry and a judicial inquiry. The administrative inquiry aims to quickly determine the technical causes of the accident, to remedy them. The purpose of the judicial inquiry is to establish the responsibilities and can therefore be a lengthier process. Let us recall that the primary purpose of the criminal trial is not to identify a culprit, but to respond to an incrimination (for manslaughter and accidental injury) which is not specific to collective accidents. This investigation is also carried out in order to explain the reasons of this accident to the victims and their relatives. And lastly, such an investigation allows access to the judge, which is a fundamental right.

Disasters tend to be complex phenomena. Faced with multiple potential causes, which could be either technical and/or human, the judge is obliged to call on expert opinion to clarify the reality. The expert report ordered by the judge must be at the service of the truth, and must enlighten the court, allow it to understand what has happened so that it can judicially establish the potential liabilities. The truth is not absolute and is fixed in the current state of science.

The administrative and the judicial inquiries complement each other. Both provide elements of research that help advance safety. The administrative report is useful to the judge. Thus, for the plane crash that occurred on March 24, 2001 in Saint-Barthélemy, the correctional court of Basse-Terre took into account the opinion issued by the experts of the BEA[1] to render its judgment of November 15, 2006.

The issues addressed in disasters cases are mostly scientific, giving a prominent place to expertise in contemporary criminal trials. These cases do not present any particular legal technicality, but show difficulties related to the technical fields covered. However, the judge is often unfamiliar with these questions. Unlike investigators and experts, they do not have any specific technical competence. Naturally, they can undertake training in order to acquire better knowledge of the field, to understand the various documents, to be able to ask the right questions, to be in a position not to be manipulated by one party or the other [6].

The expert is appointed by the judge to provide them with elements within their field of technical competence established in the sole interest of the manifestation of the truth. In all cases, the expert's performance must be of high quality and impartial. The expert does not have to rule on the merits of the case. They deliver scientific knowledge to the magistrate, but do not take part in the decision making, which falls exclusively within the jurisdiction of the judge. It is up to the judge to decide, not the expert. The conclusions of the experts are binding neither on the judges nor on the parties. The criminal judge will include in their decision the elements of the report which allow them to form a conviction. In the trial of the Mont Blanc tunnel, three experts had been appointed to determine the causes of the fire. Two of them drew on three private expert reports, one of which was paid for by the insurer of the truck.

[1]The French Bureau of Enquiry and Analysis for Civil Aviation Safety (*Bureau d'enquêtes et d'analyses*).

The theses proposed by the experts were rigorously analysed, weighed and compared with the other factual elements. The investigating judge then also sought the advice of a professor from the University of Lausanne; this last thesis was chosen because it presented no contradiction with the facts, the chronology of the events having been verified by simulation.

Disasters shed a different light on the relationship between magistrates and experts. Expertise, which should be an enlightening tool, can prove to be a delaying tool. It is necessary to be aware of the difficulties related to the limited number of specialized experts, in fields such as aviation. This may raise the issue of the independence of the experts, who might sometimes be linked in one way or another to someone who is potential responsible party for the event.

5 Conclusion

Ending the criminalization of disasters could be an excessive approach and negative for safety and security, specifically in high-risk industries. It is through criminal law that society warns its members and stresses the essential values to be protected. The judicial decision has an undeniable pedagogical function. It serves as a benchmark in the interest of risk prevention, with regards to safety actors in general, beyond the protagonists of the disaster. This approach is part of an objective to prevent the repetition of disasters and encourages a better consideration of human and organisational factors.

References

1. C. Clarkson, Corporate culpability. Web J. Curr. Leg. Issues **2** (1998)
2. M.-A. Descamps, Catastrophe et responsabilité. Revue française de sociologie **13**(3), 376–391 (1972). https://doi.org/10.2307/3320531
3. F. Desportes, F. Le Gunehec, *Droit pénal général,* vols. 798-4. Economica (2002)
4. EESC, *TEN/416* (European Economic and Social Committee, Brussels, 2010)
5. European Parliament, Regulation (EU) No 996/2010 of the European Parliament and of the Council. Off. J. Eur. Union (L 295/35) (2010), https://www.easa.europa.eu/document-library/regulations/regulation-eu-no-9962010
6. K. Favro, M. Lobe-Lobas, J.-P. Markus, in *L'expert dans tous ses états. A la recherche d'une déontologie de l'expert*, ed. by K. Favro, M. Lobe-Lobas, J.-P. Markus. Dalloz (2016)
7. Joint resolution regarding criminalization of aviation accidents (2006), www.flightsafety.org
8. Just culture (n.d.), Eurocontrol, https://www.eurocontrol.int/articles/just-culture
9. C. Lacroix, *La réparation des dommages en cas de catastrophes.* LGDJ (2008)
10. C. Lacroix, M.-F. Steinlé-Feuerbach, *La judiciarisation des grandes catastrophes - Approche comparée du recours à la justice pour la gestion des grandes catastrophes (de type accidents aériens ou ferroviaires)*, ed. by C. Lacroix, M.-F. Steinlé-Feuerbach. Dalloz (2015)

11. R. Matthews, *Blackstone's Guide to the Corporate Manslaughter and Corporate Homicide Act 2007* (Blackstone Press, 2008)
12. Ministry of Justice, *A guide to the Corporate Manslaughter and Corporate Homicide Act 2007.* UK Ministry of Justice. Crown copyright (2007)
13. D. Salas, L'éthique politique à l'épreuve du droit pénal. Revue des Sciences Criminelles **163** (2000)

Integrating Organizational and Management Variables in the Analysis of Safety and Risk

Paul R. Schulman

Abstract For decades, despite research and description of modern large-scale technologies as "socio-technical systems", there has been little headway made in integrating research on both the socio and technical aspects of these systems. Social scientists and engineers continue to have contrasting and often non-intersecting approaches to the analysis of organizational factors and the physical aspects of technologies. This essay argues that an important part of this problem has been the ambiguous and underspecified character of the social science research concepts applied to the analysis of organization and management factors. It suggests an important opportunity to more closely integrate social science research into the understanding of hazardous technologies as socio-technical systems through a strategy of clarifying concepts and definitions (such as "safety") that allow transforming qualitative organizational and managerial "factors" into variables to create metrics useful in the evaluation of safety management systems. It argues also that practitioners have an important role to play in this process. A final argument addresses the contribution that safety metrics could make to the development of higher resolution safety management across a wider spectrum of scales and time-frames than those currently considered by managers and designers of socio-technical systems.

Keywords Socio-technical system · Safety · Organizational factors · Metrics

1 A Persistent Disconnect between Organizational Aspects and Engineering

For many decades, organizational theorists, cognitive and social psychologists, political scientists, sociologists and anthropologists and science and technology studies specialists have researched technologies under the analytic framework of socio-technical systems [6]. This research has provided important insights into human factors and ergonomics [9, 29]; the psychological and anthropological aspects of

P. R. Schulman (✉)
University of California, Berkeley, USA
e-mail: paul@mills.edu

B. Journé et al. (eds.), *Human and Organisational Factors*,
SpringerBriefs in Safety Management,
https://doi.org/10.1007/978-3-030-25639-5_9

technologies [15]; the understanding of management challenges posed by complex technologies [5, 16, 22]; organizational and managerial dimensions of high reliability in the operation of hazardous technologies [1, 11, 19, 20, 23]; and, more recently, the analysis of catastrophic accidents involving complex technical systems [13, 16–18, 26]. Current accident analyses almost always identify organizational and managerial factors as root if not proximate causes of these accidents.

Yet for all of this development the research that has explored the organizational and managerial side of technical systems remains in the main un-integrated into the perspectives taken by engineers and many managers in their technical designs and organizational practices. Instead of thinking of both organizational and technical dimensions together as part of socio-technical systems, many designers and managers continue to think of humans and organizations as simple extensions of machines or as sources of error in the proper operation of technical systems. Here, for example, is one recent description of human factors engineering offered by an engineer at a safety meeting:

> If you open the plates of a circuit breaker, you will eventually have an arc. You don't want the electrons to arc, but no engineer would say that the electrons that formed the arc were lazy or complacent: if you don't want the arc, you engineer the system around the constraint. Human factors engineering operates according to the same principle; identify the constraints in the interactions between the employees and the workspaces, tools, and technology, and engineer around it.[1]

Meant to be an argument against attributing accidents simply to operator failures, this statement at the same time reveals a narrower engineering perspective. We know from socio-technical systems research that human and organizational factors can be a support to design and not only a constraint. For example, engineers may make design errors or offer incomplete designs that humans can identify, and organizations can correct. We know also that human behavior, despite its aggregate regularities, is less predictable and has more variance in particular cases than the physical laws and principles within which engineers design. Given that technologies are socio-technical systems, we should expect engineers to incorporate human and organizational factors more deeply into designs and not simply design "around them".

However, integrating organizational variables into technical design processes poses many challenges.

2 Challenges to Reconcile Them

It is not by oversight that organizational and managerial variables are often neglected, in engineering or risk research. A range of large divides exist between organizational and management research, and the performance and risk variables typically attended to by commercial organizations and the regulatory agencies that oversee

[1]Remarks made at a "Safety *en banc*" event at the California Public Utilities Commission, San Francisco, California, 19 October 2016.

them. Considering these divides will provide clues in developing strategies to achieve both a research and practical integration of social and technical variables in the understanding and practice of safety management.

2.1 Technical and Methodological Differences

Concepts and definitions of physical or mechanical variables are largely agreed-upon and formally expressed through stipulated meanings in *artificial language* such as physical descriptions or mathematical models and formulas. Most are measured along interval scales.

Social and organizational factors such as leadership, authority, centralization, decision-making, motivation, mindfulness, stress, culture and even "safety" itself are grounded in concepts expressed in *natural language* with all of its ambiguities and imprecision [7, 8]. These concepts are then difficult to translate into measurable "variables". These organizational and managerial "variables" are often defined as nominal categories (e.g. "high reliability" organizations) or described as opposites in binary pairs (e.g. flexibility/ridigity or centralization/decentralization) not as continuous scales of measurement [24]. These are "factors" but not really variables.

Further, much safety and accident research is in the form of case studies which are difficult to compare and aggregate because of their elements of uniqueness. Often the management or organizational failures are described in non standardized terms that do not allow comparative measurement. It is also difficult to learn about the impact of organizational and managerial factors across cases because without interval measures, we cannot construct regression models to determine their separate contribution to given outputs.

2.2 Practical Challenges

Because organization and management concepts are likely to be categorical and not easily expressible in ordinal or interval measures, it is difficult to connect analyses of them as factors with physical and mechanical variables for purposes of modeling integrated relationships in affecting the safety or performance of an organization. Also, many of the social sciences that analyze organizational factors are, unlike engineering, not "design sciences" with research directed toward formal design principles and cumulative findings to guide action and application.

2.3 *Political Challenges*

Finally, there are political problems with employing organizational and managerial factors in an integrated analysis of safety. Often these factors have implications that raise the political temperature surrounding their development and use. Business organizations may resist leadership, decision-making or culture analyses because of their potential implications for assessments of managerial competence or effectiveness. Regulatory organizations may avoid using organizational and managerial findings because of their vulnerability to political or legal challenges if they base regulations and enforcements on what will be challenged as ambiguous or subjective measures and assessments.

How, given the diverse analytic domains of physical models versus organizational factors, do we find a way to combine them in an *additive* way to improve our understanding, management and regulation of safety and risk in complex technical systems? Important risks and opportunities call for closer integration between the two research approaches, but we are currently far away from this objective, with a mutual ignorance, indifference, or even hostility, between researchers in these two domains. The recent stress on safety management systems (SMS's) by industry groups and regulators has created growing demand for careful analysis of the implementation of these systems and the measurement of their impact on rates of incidents and accidents. How can we address these opportunities?

3 The Need for Clarifying Key Concepts

Among the key organizational concepts that lack clarity is the concept of *safety itself*, and the relationship between safety and risk. For many designers, managers and regulators, it is all too often assumed that "safety" is synonymous with the mitigation of risk. "*How much safety are we willing to pay for*?" is often a question about "*Which specific risks are we willing to address?*" But a report on aviation safety by a group of representatives from 18 national aviation regulatory agencies concluded the following:

> Safety is more than the absence of risk; it requires specific systemic enablers of safety to be maintained at all times to cope with the known risks, [and] to be well prepared to cope with those risks that are not yet known [21].

Safety is about assurance; risk is about loss. Safety is in many respects a perceptual property, "*defined and measured more by its absence than its presence*" [18]. It is hard to establish definitively that things are "safe", but much easier to recognize specific conditions of "unsafety" retrospectively in the face of accidents. Risk is a calculated property. Several failures or incidents can occur without invalidating a risk estimate (two 100-year storms in consecutive years for example), but a single failure can disconfirm the assumption of safety. This distinction also applies to a difference between safety management and risk management. Risk management is managing to probability estimations which apply to events over a large run-of-operations or number of years. Safety management is managing down to the level of precluding a single event in a single operation at any time [3].

Karl Weick's definition of safety as "*the continuous production of dynamic non-events*" [28] offers more promise. Here "safety" defines positive actions—identifying potential sources and consequences of accidents (including incomplete or unforgiving technical designs), acting to prevent them, constantly monitoring for precursor conditions that add risk or uncertainty, training and planning for the containment of consequences of accidents if they do happen—in short *safety management.* As part of this definition, it is important to understand the distinction between safety as "dynamic non-events" and non-events in systems without careful management that simply have so far "failed to fail". Unfortunately, there is at present significant confusion about this conceptual difference. How can we distinguish non-events that are simply "failing to fail" from those dynamic non-events that reflect effective safety management, without having to wait for an accident? The answer partly lies with understanding and measuring the implementation process of safety management systems.

4 Some Propositions about the Implementation of Safety Management Systems

There is an important difference between implementing the structural features of an SMS in an organization—safety officers; safety plans; formal meetings; safety budgets; formal accountability and reporting relationships—and

- achieving a widely distributed acceptance of safety management as an integral part of actual jobs in the organization,
- a collectively shared set of assumptions and values concerning safety (a "safety culture") and
- commitment to safety as part of the individual identity of personnel in an organization.

Without wide and deep employee engagement, an SMS will simply be an administrative artifact without a strong connection to actual behaviors that link to safety-promoting performance and safer outcomes. Further, it takes time, persistent effort, adaptive behavior, *continuous monitoring* (with metrics) and correction to implement and maintain an effective SMS.

These propositions lead us back then to the earlier essential question about determining the effectiveness of a safety management system, without having to wait for an accident. One answer is to develop metrics to detect the full implementation and integrity in operation of an SMS:

- metrics for organizational and managerial conditions and practices—both positive and negative—that give information about the condition of safety management itself [10, 21, 25] and
- metrics identifying and addressing precursor management to add granularity to safety performance assessments apart from accidents.

4.1 A Strategy for SMS Metrics Development

Retrospective measures already exist for incidents and accidents, many required by law and regulation. The strategy of SMS metrics is to provide *precursor* indicators so that the integrity of an SMS can be assessed before an accident occurs.

The precursor strategy is well illustrated by research on "High Reliability Organizations" (HROs) such as selected nuclear power plants, air traffic control organizations, high voltage electrical grids that were known for effective safety management [11, 12, 19, 20]. This HRO research led to the recognition that a key to high reliability is not a rigid invariance in operations and technical and organizational conditions, but rather the management of fluctuations in task performance and conditions which keeps them within acceptable bandwidths and outside of dangerous or unstudied conditions [23]. Supporting this narrow bandwidth management is the careful identification, analysis, and exclusion of precursor conditions that could lead to accidents or failures. HROs begin with those core events and accidents they wish never to experience and then analyze outward to conditions both physical and organizational that could, along given chains of causation, lead ultimately to these accidents or to significantly increased probabilities of them. This "precursor zone" typically grows outward to include additional precursor conditions based on more careful analysis and experience. These precursors are *leading* indicators, for these organizations, of potential failures and are given attention and addressed by supervisors and managers. Precursors are in effect "weak signals" to which "receptors" throughout many levels of the organization are attuned and sensitive. In its effectiveness, a process of precursor management with metrics can impart a special kind of "precursor resilience" to organizations [20]. With an effective safety management system, they can move back from the approach to precursor zones quickly and still maintain the robustness of safe performance and reliable outputs.

Metrics should reflect *models of causation* pertaining to safety. It should be clear why they are important as metrics. This is promoted by the leading indicator strategy and its underlying analysis. The identification of precursors through their potential connection to accidents provides validity to them as metrics.

Single, high-value metrics offer perverse incentives to "manage to the metric" or to distort the measurement process itself. Or as one manager once conceded, "*organizations will do what you inspect but not necessarily what you expect!*" More metrics with more data if possible should then be developed to cover each element of a safety management system to be assessed and improve the overall reliability of the process.

Finally, safety management metrics should be widely accepted in an organization as important tools for learning, not as instruments of control and punishment. To promote their acceptance, they should be the product of a joint development process which includes regulators, organizational researchers and participants at a variety of levels and across departments and units. Individuals at the level of task performance often have tacit knowledge and practical insights about conditions that support or detract from their safe performance and measurements, both direct and indirect, that can reveal these conditions. The metrics that are developed should make sense to all participants.

4.2 *Achieving Higher Resolution Safety Management*

The integration of SMS metrics with physical and engineering analyses can lead to a more powerful socio-technical understanding of complex systems, their operation and their risks. But coupling this understanding to safety requires also that we increase the *scale*, *scope* and *time frame* of safety management itself. Here are some examples.

4.2.1 Shifts in Scale: Micro-analysis

Many precursors to system failures can be found in conditions that surround the performance of specialized tasks. Human factors research addresses some of these—including attention load, noise levels, ergonomic requirements that induce fatigue or injury. More recently cognitive work analysis research has focused on micro-level task psychology, sub-cultures and roles associated with successful task performance relative to particular technologies or missions [14, 27]. For example, robotic surgery has led to changes in the roles of surgeons and support groups and requires personal resilience among surgeons to deal with unexpected issues as well as new methods for surgical training [2].

A similar micro-analysis has also been applied to understanding the role of "reliability professionals" prominent in the operation of HROs [19, 20]. These are individuals who have special perspectives on safety and reliability, cognitively and normatively. They mix formal deductive knowledge and experiential knowledge in their understanding of the systems they operate and manage. Their view of the "system" is larger than their formal roles and job descriptions, and frequently center on real-time activities. They internalize norms and invest their identity in the reliable and safe operation of their systems. In this they are "professionals" on behalf of reliability and safety, but not defined by particular degrees or certifications.

This degree of granularity allows the identification of SMS implementation down to the level asserted as important in the first proposition: to be successful it must include achieving a widely distributed acceptance of safety management and safety culture as an integral part of actual jobs down to the level of specific tasks. Micro-level analyses can lead to metrics that can be indicators of this degree of implementation. Note that the shift to this micro level also means an analysis of actions and behaviors over short-time intervals, in the real-time operation of a technical system.

4.2.2 Shifts in Scale: Macro-analysis

At the other end of high resolution is the ability to analyze actions and behaviors over larger scales and scope and with effects over considerably longer time intervals. Here the analysis and measurement would move beyond a single organization and its SMS to cover network safety and reliability [4]. This leads to a consideration of safety management in relation to interconnected risks among infrastructures [20] and across sectors.

Transmission planning for large utility grids, for example, is a process that can cut across large populations and across nations. Generally, it has to look ahead over a 5–10-year time frame to anticipate electricity demand patterns and new generation technologies as well as to encompass the time it takes to translate plans into actual construction of new transmission lines and capacity. But as one grid management analyst noted: "*What goes on in planning eventually ends up in operations.*" That is, activity and management on this time frame will eventually impose itself on day-to-day real-time grid operations.

4.2.3 Elongated Time Frames

Many interconnected risks span an international and even a global scale and an inter-generational time-frame. Problems such as global climate change and sea-level rise are slow-motion issues which convey inter-generational risk. These safety management problems will need to be addressed across many different sectors on a global scale over the next 20–50 years.

Similarly, long term effects of nuclear waste disposition and storage are safety management challenges. But they require planning and possibly ongoing safety management attention over decades, if not centuries. We currently pay attention to planning for reliability of infrastructures, but we will have to pay more attention, with metrics, to reliable planning itself as a management process. Larger scales and longer time frames also require that safety management be supported by social policy and regulation.

Analyses of safety management across these scales and time frames can lead to a higher resolution additive understanding of organizational and managerial factors in safety and reliability, running from macro to micro levels of analysis over long- and short-term-time frames. Then we can analyze the safety interconnections between the levels and time scales—how what happens or does not happen at one level of planning and management scale can affect the safety of operating conditions at another. How culture, roles and psychology surrounding individuals in their specific tasks can

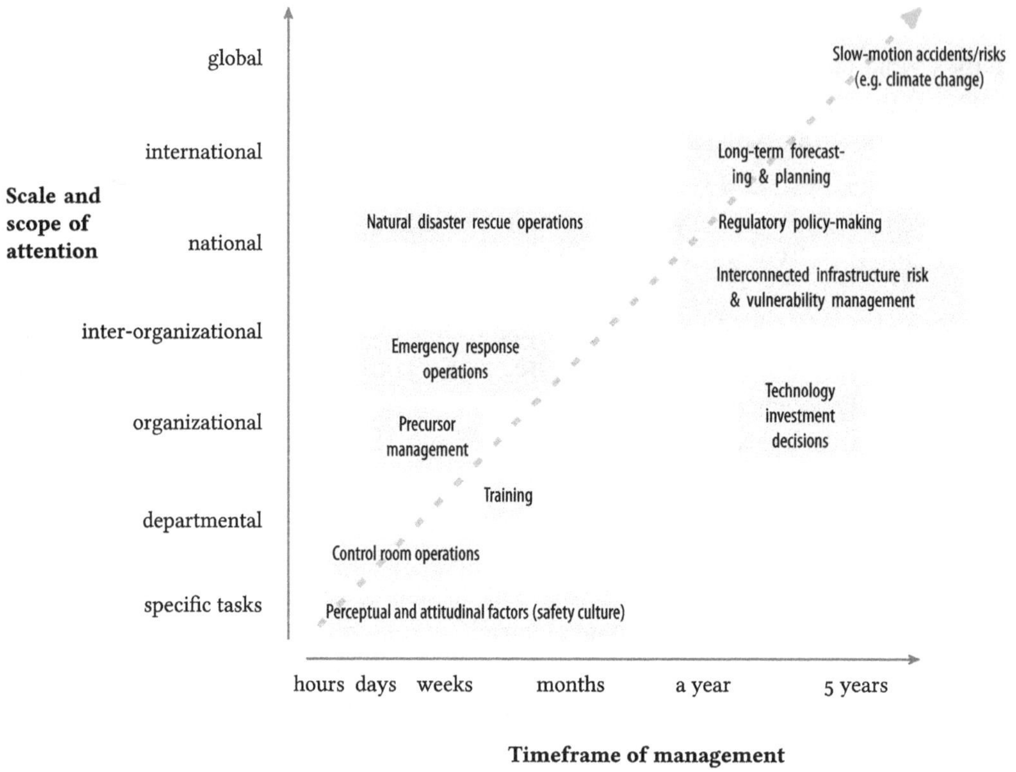

Fig. 1 A higher resolution safety management framework

affect their performance and how this performance in turn impacts system safety well beyond that task. The following figure (see Fig. 1) is one integrated illustration of the scale and scope of organizational and managerial attention in relation to the time frame needed for action to promote safety.

5 Conclusion

This paper began with an expression of disappointment over the lack of progress in integrating organizational and management variables with physical models into our understanding of technologies as socio-technical systems.

It concludes with the recognition that it will take a large and persistent R&D effort to achieve the integration of organizational and managerial variables as safety management metrics into the physical analysis of technical systems. But an integrated understanding of socio-technical systems, across scales, scopes and time, could significantly add to our understanding of how to manage and ultimately design them for increased safety.

References

1. R. Amalberti, The paradoxes of almost totally safe transport systems. Saf. Sci. **37**, 109–126 (2001)
2. M. Beane, Shadow learning: building robotic surgical skill when approved means fail. Adm. Sci. Q. (2018). http://journals.sagepub.com/doi/full/10.1177/0001839217751692
3. C. Danner, P. Schulman, Rethinking risk assessment for public utility safety regulation. Risk Anal. (2018). https://www.researchgate.net/publication/328988807_Rethinking_Risk_Assesment_for_Public_Utility_Safety_Regulation_Public_Utility_Safety_Regulation
4. M. De Bruijne, *Networked Reliability: Institutional Fragmentation and the Reliability of Service Provision in Critical Infrastructures* (Delft University of Technology, Delft, 2006)
5. S. Dekker, *Drifting Into Failure* (CRC Press, Boca Raton, 2011)
6. F.E. Emery, *Characteristics of Socio-technical Systems* (Tavistock Documents, London, 1959), p. 527
7. J. Gerring, What makes a concept good? A criterial framework for understanding concept formation. Polity **31**(3), 357–393 (1999)
8. J. Gerring, P. Baressi, Putting ordinary language to work: a mini-max strategy for concept formation in the social sciences. J. Theor. Polit. **15**(2), 201–232 (2003)
9. R.J.B. Hutton, L.G. Militello, Applied cognitive task analysis (ACTA). Ergonomics **41**(11), 1618–1641 (1998)
10. INPO, Traits of a healthy nuclear safety culture (2012)
11. T. LaPorte, High reliability organizations: unlikely, demanding and at risk. J. Contingencies Crisis Manag. **4**(2), 60–71 (1996)
12. T. LaPorte, P. Consolini, Working in practice but not in theory: theoretical challenges of high reliability organizations. Public Adm. Res. Theory **1**(1), 19–47 (1991)
13. Z. Medvedev, *The Truth About Chernobyl* (Basic Books, New York, 1991)
14. N. Naikar, Cognitive work analysis: an influential legacy extending beyond human factors and engineering. Appl. Ergon. **59**, 528–540 (2017)
15. C. Perin, *Shouldering Risk: The Culture of Control in the Nuclear Power Industry* (Princeton University Press, Princeton, 2004)
16. C. Perrow, *Normal Accidents* (Princeton University Press, Princeton, 1999)
17. President's Commission on the Accident at Three-Mile Island, U.S. Government Printing Office, Washington, D. C. (1979)
18. J. Reason, *Organizational Accidents Revisited* (CRC Press, Boca Raton, 2016)
19. E. Roe, P. Schulman, *High Reliability Management* (Stanford University Press, Stanford, 2008)
20. E. Roe, P. Schulman, *Reliability and Risk: The Challenge of Managing Interconnected Critical Infrastructures* (Stanford University Press, Stanford, 2016)
21. Safety Management International Collaboration Group, *Safety management system evaluation tool* (2013), https://www.skybrary.aero/bookshelf/books/1774.pdf
22. S. Sagan, *The Limits of Safety* (Princeton University Press, Princeton, 1995)
23. P. Schulman, The negotiated order of organizational reliability. Adm. Soc. **25**(3), 353–372 (1993)
24. S. Stevens, On the theory of scales of measurement. Science **103**, 677–680 (1946)
25. U.L., Using leading and lagging safety indicators to manage workplace health and safety risk. Underwriters Laboratories (2013)
26. D. Vaughan, *The Challenger Launch Decision* (University of Chicago Press, Chicago, 2016)
27. K.J. Vicente, *Cognitive Work Analysis* (Lawrence Erlbaum Associates, Mahwah, 1999)
28. K. Weick, Organizing for transient reliability: the production of dynamic non-events. J. Contingencies Crisis Manag. **19**, 21–27 (2011)
29. K.M. Wilson, W.S. Helton, M.W. Wiggins, Cognitive engineering. Cogn. Sci. **4**(1), 17–31 (2013)

Turning the Management of Safety Risk into a Business Function: The Challenge for Industrial Sociotechnical Systems in the 21st Century

Daniel Mauriño

Abstract Since World War II, the history of safety in industrial sociotechnical systems has evolved through different paradigms. From the days of "operate-break-fix-operate", through system safety, human factors, organizational factors and "cognition in the wild", engineering and social disciplines have contributed to the safety of industrial systems that require close interaction between people and technology to achieve their production goals. Yet, regardless of paradigms, disciplines or industries, the hierarchical status of safety has remained largely unaltered: safety may be claimed to be the first priority of industrial systems, but boardrooms agendas seldom reflect that assertion. The contention in this chapter is that if safety is to elevate its status within other functions in industrial systems, if it is to become an out-of-the-ordinary topic on boardrooms agendas, it must contribute to the management of overall organizational risk, along the same lines and at the same level as the financial, legal, quality, human resources or any other business functions of the organization. The chapter provides a conceptual outline of the building blocks of a system that would contribute towards such an end. Central to this system is its capability to support an evidence-based allocation of prioritized safety resources, as well as the use of procedures and a language that parallels the procedures and the language of other business functions. The chapter builds on and mostly discusses the experience of the aviation industry, because it is the sector that has, until now, taken a lead in the direction proposed. Nevertheless, it is asserted that the notion of the management of safety as a business function is transversal to all industrial sociotechnical systems.

Keywords Accident risk reduction · Business management · Human factors · Management · Risk · Safety management · Safety risk management · Sociotechnical systems · System safety

D. Mauriño (✉)
Independent Safety Management Consultant, Milton, ON, Canada
e-mail: daniel.maurino@gmail.com

B. Journé et al. (eds.), *Human and Organisational Factors*,
SpringerBriefs in Safety Management,
https://doi.org/10.1007/978-3-030-25639-5_10

1 Introduction

The proposal to turn the management of safety (or safety management) into a business function hinges around three key ideas that apply regardless of the industry and across the typical range of conditions under which industrial sociotechnical systems operate and deliver their services.

First, safety must evolve from its historical role—without abandoning it –, which was almost exclusively focused on accident risk reduction, and broaden into a function that contributes to the overall risk management of the organization. To this end, it becomes necessary to develop processes and activities for the management of safety risk (or safety risk management) that mirror the processes and activities for the management of risk in other functions that support overall risk management.

Second, it is almost impossible for industrial systems to address all the safety concerns that they face during their service delivery operations: the cherished notion of zero accidents is closer to an idealized concept than to a realistic possibility. Therefore, industrial systems must prioritize safety concerns through the anticipated management of safety risk, in a manner consistent with the prioritization of risk of other business functions, rather than "run after the last accident" while requesting, after the fact, limitless resources to avoid repetition.

Third, involvement in decision-making regarding the management of safety risk must move up the organizational ladder—as does involvement in decision-making regarding the management of risk in other business functions—from the subject matter expert level to executive leadership level.

The chapter starts by providing a brief account of the disciplines that nurtured safety in industrial socio-technical systems after World War II. This is because a proposal based on evolutionary change is essential, given the documented abhorrence for revolutionary change of socio-technical systems. Following this account, the chapter develops a conceptual proposal for a system for the management of safety risk as a business function, and briefly discusses—as the cornerstone of the proposal—a particular perspective on the notions of management and risk. The chapter lastly discusses the three key ideas outlined above, as the vehicles turn—in practice—the management of safety into a business function.

2 Brief Historical Background

2.1 System Safety

System safety was the first post-World War II contributor to industrial systems safety and remains, after more than 60 years, the reference for technological industrial design regardless of industry [3]. Two footnotes regarding the potential of system safety to contribute to the management of safety as a business function are relevant here. First, system safety was conceived exclusively for the improvement of *technical* systems (an aircraft, ship, car, engine, pump, etc.). Second, within the strong engineering credo of system safety, the human operator is considered a liability, due to the potential for human mishandling of technology during service delivery operations.

2.2 Human Factors

Human factors joined system safety in contributing to industrial systems safety *circa* 1970s [6]. Three footnotes are relevant here. Human factors was conceived for application to *socio-technical* systems, of which industrial systems are prime examples. Second, from the cognitive perspective, human factors considers the human operator an asset, due to the ability of humans to "think on their feet" and provide responses to operational situations unforeseen by design and planning [2, 5, 10]. Third, from the organizational perspective, human factors considers human error as a symptom of deficiencies in the architecture of the system rather than the cause: operational error is an indication of problem(s), but not the problem(s) itself [8].

2.3 Business Management

Until business management appeared in industrial safety, some twenty-five years ago, the paradigmatic safety goalpost had been the absence of low frequency, high-severity events: safety was viewed as freedom from accidents. Under business management thinking applied to safety—"*one cannot manage what one cannot measure*"—it is necessary to prospect higher frequency, lower severity events as alternative safety goalposts that provide the larger volume of data necessary for the development of safety risk management information. Business management applied to safety also leads the organization to assign sense to the safety dollar: is the safety return worth the resources invested for its achievement?

Two final footnotes are relevant here. It is intrinsic to business management that the organization must develop multiple sources of information acquisition during service delivery operations. Accident investigation as the sole source of safety data does not generate the volume (or the calibre) of information necessary for the management of safety risk. Second, business management applied to safety does not aim at an "ideal" safety status (*safety first*, *zero accidents*, *safety is everybody's business*, *safety starts at the top*, and so forth), but at service delivery operations under conditions of "acceptable" (i.e. controlled) safety risk.

3 A System for the Management of Safety Risk as a Business Function

3.1 A Conceptual Proposal

The proposal for a system for the management of safety risk as a business function builds upon the integration of aspects from system safety, human factors and business management.

From system safety, the proposal retains the two basic entities of hazard and risk and introduces a third entity: potential consequence (the anticipated outcome of hazards). This provides guidance for the capture of high frequency, low severity safety concerns in a volume appropriate to the need of "measuring what must be managed," and to support the evaluation of the safety concerns for prioritization purposes.

From human factors, the proposal retains organizational psychology (the organizational accident) and cognitive psychology (human performance as an asset rather than a liability) as central linchpins. These provide guidance to define the context where the capture of information on hazards takes place and allows a perspective of operational human performance *vis-à-vis* features of the workplace that may negatively affect it. From this perspective, it is essential not to lose sight of the fact that "work as imagined" (procedures) and "work as delivered" (practices) are frequently asymmetrical. Since operations are delivered according to practices and not procedures, the implications of this asymmetry in industrial systems service delivery operations safety become clear [9].

The integration of elements from system safety and human factors covers two of the central activities in the management of safety risk as a business function: *hazard identification and analysis* and *safety risk evaluation and mitigation*.

From business management, the proposal retains the three basic elements of organizational control theory (direction, supervision and control) to monitor the effectiveness of the mitigations implemented for the management of safety risk. The result is the third central activity in the management of safety risk as a business function: *safety performance monitoring* using safety performance indicators and safety performance targets.

Interfacing hazard identification and analysis with safety risk evaluation and mitigation and with safety performance monitoring, conforms to a process known as *safety risk management*, which is the conceptual basis for the management of safety as a business function [7].

3.2 The Terms Management and Risk

A conceptual proposal for a system for the management of safety risk as a business function cannot avoid a discussion of the terms *management* and *risk*. These terms are common currency in the safety language of industrial systems; yet, they are often applied in a colloquial sense.

The term *management* derives from the early Italian verb *maneggiare*, meaning, "*to ride a horse with skill*" [4]. At face value, the meaning appears as an irrelevant metaphor. However, riding a horse with skill requires directing, supervising and controlling the horse so that it does what the rider wants in order to reach the intended destination. From this angle, the implications of the etymology of the term in providing *direction*, *supervision* and *control* to safety risk management activities become explicit.

The term *risk* also derives from an early Italian verb: *risicare*, meaning, "*to dare*" [1]. As the etymology of the term suggests, risk is not about fate but about decision and choice: we decide to accept or reject the choice(s) resulting from the evaluation of risk.

Combining the two terms into a single clause—risk management—and drawing from their respective etymologies, it is proposed that risk management involves *daring to make decisions about choices that provide direction, supervision and control to specific activities*. Extending this to safety, *safety* risk management involves daring to make decisions about choices that provide direction, supervision and control to *safety* activities.

Risk is not limited to safety; risk may be related to finance, legal, economics, quality or any other function of an industrial system. In fact, the term *enterprise risk* has been coined to encompass the overall risks faced by an industrial system, and to underline the importance of their joint management.

The joint management of overall enterprise risk—enterprise risk management—is important because it ensures the continued viability of an organization. Thus, the management of safety risk through a dedicated management system goes beyond accident risk prevention, to become a contributor to organizational viability. Safety risk management is therefore the essential business function to be delivered by the safety structure of the industrial system to support enterprise risk management.

4 Three Key Ideas for a System for the Management of Safety Risk as a Business Function

4.1 Safety beyond Accident Risk Reduction: Direction and Supervision

The first key idea for operationalizing a system for the management of safety risk as a business function focuses on the need to broaden the scope of the safety function in industrial systems and acknowledge the difference between accident risk reduction (the term commonly used by industrial systems is *accident prevention*) and safety risk management. This is a difference that goes beyond semantics.

Accident risk reduction/accident prevention involves activities to avoid experiencing low-probability/high severity negative outcomes. The link between accident risk reduction activities and the avoidance of accidents is explicit and direct.

Safety risk management involves activities that generate information to support the choice of senior leaders regarding priorities in the allocation of resources to address potential consequences of hazards. The link between safety risk management activities and the avoidance of accidents is implicit and indirect.

There is a likelihood that safety risk management may prevent accidents. This would be a by-product—as opposed to a goal—of safety risk management. Accident risk avoidance is the province of safety programmes. Safety risk management is the vehicle for a system for the management of safety risk as a business function. Safety programmes are resourced, or *not* resourced, as a function of choices in the priorities regarding the allocation of resources that result from safety risk management information.

It is worth emphasising this point: safety risk management is about decisions on priorities regarding the allocation of resources (including the decision to *not* allocate resources) to contribute to the management of overall enterprise risk.

Applying the three basic elements of organizational control theory to the management of safety risk just as they apply to the management of financial, quality, human resources or any other risk within an industrial system provides:

- *Direction,* by setting risk management targets; in this case, safety performance targets;
- *Supervision,* through the collection and analysis of information regarding risk monitoring indicators; in this case, safety performance indicators; and
- *Control*, through the allocation/re-allocation of resources based on the analysis of information, to achieve the risk management targets that have been set; in this case, monitoring progress of safety performance indicators towards their associated safety performance targets.

In developing safety performance indicators and safety performance targets, there should be less focus on the use of *outcomes* and more emphasis on the *parameters* that are the forerunners of the outcomes. The following example is taken from the aviation industry.

Aircraft must respect what is known as a "stable approach" to landing. Unstable approaches may lead to a number of undesirable outcomes and are a quintessential safety concern in aviation.

To conform to stable approach criteria, aircraft must be within specified position(s) of the flight controls and the landing gear, at specified indicated speed(s), and at specified engine(s) regime(s)—all this encompassed under the term "configuration"—at fixed points along the approach to the runway. These fixed points typically are 10 miles from touchdown; the final approach fix (or FAF), and the point in which the flight crew must decide whether to continue to land or initiate another approach if the approach is not stable ("the window").

The safety risk management activities involved in this example would be:

- Implementing *mitigations* that aim at ensuring that flight crews and aircraft meet the requirements to conform to stable approaches
- Providing *direction* for *monitoring* the effectiveness of mitigations by establishing safety performance targets
  - Expected aircraft configuration at 10 nautical miles from touchdown;
  - Expected aircraft configuration at the FAF; and
  - Expected aircraft configuration at "the window".
- Providing *supervision* for *measuring* the effectiveness of mitigations by establishing safety performance indicators
  - Aircraft configuration *values* at 10 nautical miles from touchdown;
  - Aircraft configuration *values* at the FAF;
  - Aircraft configuration *values* at "the window".
- Providing *control* by allocating/reallocating resources if measurement of the safety performance targets indicates that implemented mitigations fall short of achieving the expected results (expected aircraft configuration values are not met). Control is further discussed in an example from another industry in the following section.

It must be emphasized that safety risk management involves the monitoring and measurement of the *parameters* (the configuration values) underlying proposed mitigation(s), as opposed to monitoring the *outcome* that the mitigation(s) seeks to avoid (unstable approaches).

Monitoring parameters will generate a larger amount of data than monitoring outcomes, and capture information regarding the *success* of the mitigation(s) (number of flights that *do* meet stable approach criteria) rather than the *failure* of the mitigation(s) (number of flights that *do not* meet stable approach criteria). Comparing rate of success to rate of failure allows a relationship to be established between safety achievement and the investment required for the safety achievement (return on investment). Data about failure (unstable approaches) would make it difficult to establish this relationship.

4.2 The Prioritization of Safety Concerns: Control

The second key idea for developing a system for the management of safety as a business function refers to "rationing" always-finite resources, since no organization has enough resources to address all the potential consequences of hazards. This responds to the third element of organizational control theory: control.

The first step in "rationing" involves evaluating the safety risk of the potential consequences of hazards identified. Once potential consequences are safety-risk prioritized, implementation of safety risk mitigations according to determined priorities follows. As part of the prioritization, some of the potential consequences may be ignored due to resource availability, but this would be a data-supported choice.

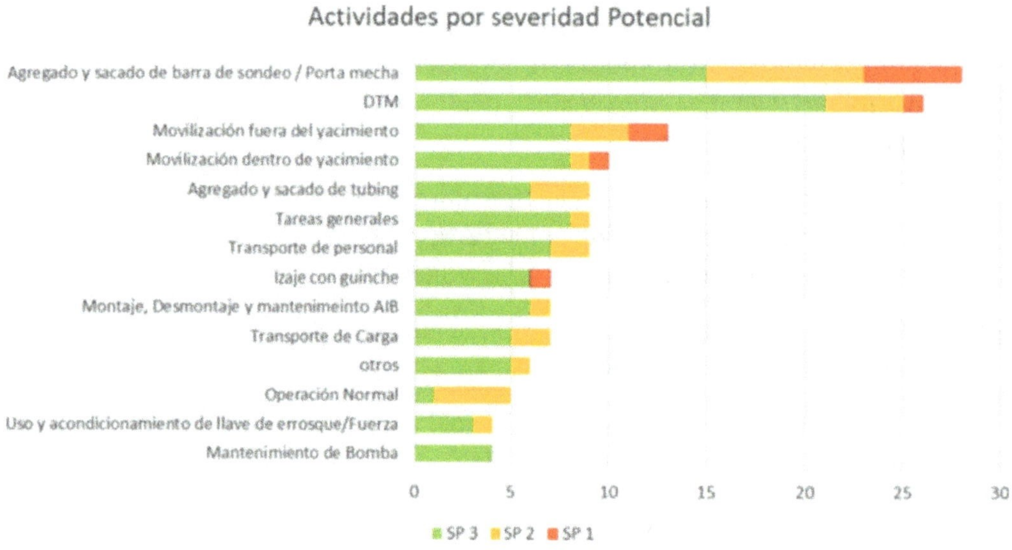

Fig. 1 Activities evaluated for safety risk

Mitigation does not automatically mean solution, and resources allocated to mitigations that do not result in the expected solutions are wasted resources that could be re-allocated for more efficient purposes (no return on investment). Thus, the second step in the "rationing" involves monitoring the effectiveness of mitigations—as close to real time as possible—to ensure the mitigations are delivering the expected safety performances (return on investment).

The aeronautical example in the previous section applies here; however, for broader illustrative purposes, a further example borrowed from the oil industry follows. The example also supports the assertion in this chapter that the management of safety as a business function travels quite well across inter-industry boundaries.

Figure 1 depicts the main safety concerns specific to an operation, risk-evaluated and prioritized according to potential severity of the consequence of the concern.[1] The nature of the safety concerns is irrelevant for the purpose of the example; what is relevant is that only 10% of the total resources available to address all safety concerns in the list were allocated to address the two with the greatest potential severity (the two top bars), meaning this operation allocates 90% of its budgeted resources to addressing lesser safety concerns. This does not necessarily mean ineffective accident risk reduction activities (i.e. ineffective accident prevention), but rather that control of safety resources (safety risk management) is not as effective as it could be. Control of safety resources not based on safety risk management may lead an organization to invest in activities that do not bring return on investment. This is often the case when resource allocation is based in opinion instead of data.

[1]English translation of this graph is irrelevant since the activities it refers to are very industry-specific. What this graph aims to convey, is the prioritization of the activities according to their safety risk evaluation.

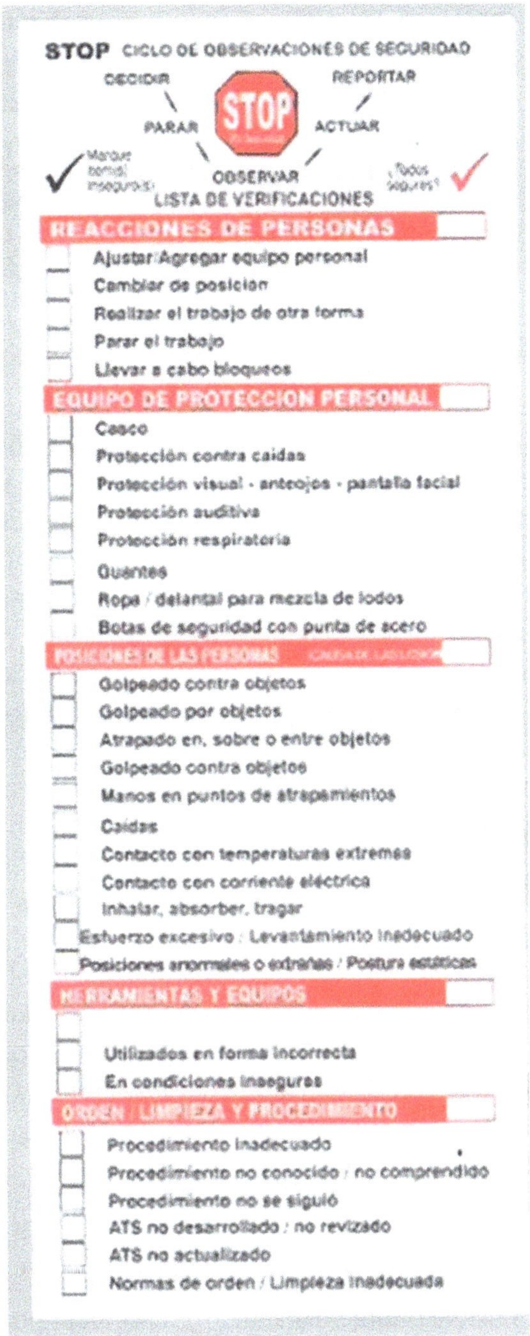

Fig. 2 Standard observation card

Moving on with the example, Fig. 2 illustrates an observation card, typical of many industries, used to routinely monitor workplace safety practices and conditions. Observation cards reflect—in theory—organizational expectations of where the most severe incidents are likely to occur during service delivery operations. In both cases illustrated above, the contents of the card and the budget allocation to risk prevention were based on personal experience, anecdotal evidence, history and so forth, and not on data. Indeed, in the example of the safety card above, closer inspection showed that nothing related to the two actions with the highest severity were reflected in the aspects to be observed. Since observations are labour-intensive, this raises questions not only related to safety, but also related to the allocation (or rather the mis-allocation) of resources.

4.3 Elevating Safety to the Boardroom

The third key idea for operationalizing a system for the management of safety risk as a business function addresses the need to elevate safety to the boardroom. This is because decisions on risk *evaluation* are purely *technical* and belong at the subject matter expert level; decisions on risk *mitigation* are *financial, legal* and *administrative* because risk mitigation involves financial, legal and administrative considerations (and costs). As such, decisions on risk mitigation belong—ultimately—in the leadership levels.

Attempts to insert safety into the routine agenda of the leadership from the accident prevention angle are self-defeating, because risk management is part of the procedures and the language of leadership; accident prevention is not. As the history of industrial systems shows, few things are more counterproductive than trying to "force safety down the throat" of leadership, trying to capture its attention by resorting to the moral and ethical undertones assigned to safety or, even worse, trying to turn leadership into safety experts.

As long as accidents do not occur, safety is not part of the routine agenda of the leadership, and rightly so: why and how could the leadership address something that has not happened? How can absence be risk-evaluated and risk-managed? An accident is to safety what bankruptcy is to finance. No financial officer would consider reporting financial success by stating that the organization has avoided bankruptcy. Yet, safety officers consistently report safety success by stating that the organization has avoided accidents.

The proposal of the chapter in this respect is simple and straightforward: if the safety function is to be effectively elevated to the boardroom, if leadership is to be encouraged into regularly making decisions regarding safety risk mitigation as part of its agenda, safety must take some distance from accident prevention and observe the procedures and the language of safety risk management. This will provide for a natural forum for safety—alongside finance, legal, quality, human resources or any of the other functions—in the organization's senior governance decision-making structure.

Are there significant roadblocks to the management of safety as a business function? Only two are envisioned. One relates to traditional mindsets among safety practitioners who mostly have engineering backgrounds, and how to modify deeply-rooted safety practices. The "changing of the guard" regarding professional demographics and the education they are receiving will facilitate removal of this potential roadblock. The other relates to data storage and retrieval. Only aviation has an industry-wide accepted taxonomy, and data management without taxonomy may quickly become a nightmare. By no means an insurmountable roadblock, it only requires minds and subject matter expertise to come together, while remembering that consensus regarding taxonomy definition is labour-intensive and it takes time, as the experience of the aviation industry indicates.

5 Conclusion

Since World War II, industrial safety has progressed under the guidance provided by three unconnected disciplines: system safety, human factors, and business management. To overcome perceived shortcomings in doing more of the same with more intensity in pursuing industrial safety in the 21st Century, the three disciplines must converge towards a point of confluence. The result of this confluence would be, in practice, the vehicle for the operationalization of the management of safety risk as a business function. The challenge ahead becomes the coordinated integration of the three disciplines into a coherent whole. This chapter has presented an outline of the integration.

References

1. G. Alston, *How Safe Is Safe Enough?* (Ashgate, Aldershot, 2003)
2. R. Amalberti, *La conduite de systèmes à risques* (Presses Universitaires de France, Paris, 1996)
3. C.A. Ericson II, The four laws of safety. J. Syst. Saf. **2007**, 8–11 (2006)
4. C. Hood, D.K.C. Jones, *Accident and Design—Contemporary Debates in Risk Management* (UCL Press, London, 1996)
5. E. Hutchins, *Cognition in the Wild* (The MIT Press, Cambridge, 2000)
6. International Civil Aviation Organization, Human Factors Training Manual. ICAO (1998)
7. D. Mauriño, Why safety management systems? International Transport Forum (ITF)/Organization for Economic Cooperation and Development (OECD) (2017), https://www.itf-oecd.org/safety-management-systems-roundtable
8. J.T. Reason, *Managing the Risks of Organizational Accidents* (Ashgate, Aldershot, 1997)
9. S.A. Snook, *Friendly Fire* (Princeton University Press, New Jersey, 2000)
10. D.D. Woods, S. Dekker, R. Cook, L. Johannesen, N. Sarter, *Behind Human Error* (Ashgate, Aldershot, 2010)

The Strategic Agility Gap: How Organizations Are Slow and Stale to Adapt in Turbulent Worlds

David D. Woods

Abstract How can organizations cope with accelerating change in more complex worlds? The growth of capabilities produces expanded scales of operation, extensive interdependencies, new vulnerabilities, and puzzling failures. The result is the strategic agility gap where organizations are *slow and stale* in recognizing changing risks and fall behind the pace of change. The chapter addresses what factors drive the gap and what adaptive capabilities allow organizations to flourish in the gap. The result is a new paradigm for continuous adaptability illustrated in web-powered enterprises.

Keywords Resilience engineering · Strategic agility gap · High reliability organizations · Complex adaptive systems (Human) · Fluency law · Web operations · Continuous adaptability

1 Introduction

Organizations face the challenge of how to adapt to the increasing pace of change in more complex worlds. The growth of capability brings rapid changes to society as *new opportunities arise, complexities grow, and new threats emerge*. The impact of deploying new technological capabilities has led to expanded scales of operation, dramatic new capabilities, extensive and hidden interdependencies, intensified pressures, new vulnerabilities, and puzzling failures.

Can organizations *keep pace* with the trajectory of change? Experience across industries indicates organizations are *slow and stale* in adapting to new threats, as well as to seize new opportunities. Surprising failures and service outages are regular occurrences in the news. One example is the threat of ransomware which offsets the value brought by new levels of computerized connectivity. This threat arose quickly with attacks on hospitals in 2016/2017 (CedarSinai/Medstar in US; Wannacry attack in the UK). Computer connectivity provided value that led to increased reliance, but also provided means for others to hijack the capability for their purposes. As

D. D. Woods (✉)
The Ohio State University, Columbus, USA
e-mail: woods.2@osu.edu

B. Journé et al. (eds.), *Human and Organisational Factors*, SpringerBriefs in Safety Management,
https://doi.org/10.1007/978-3-030-25639-5_11

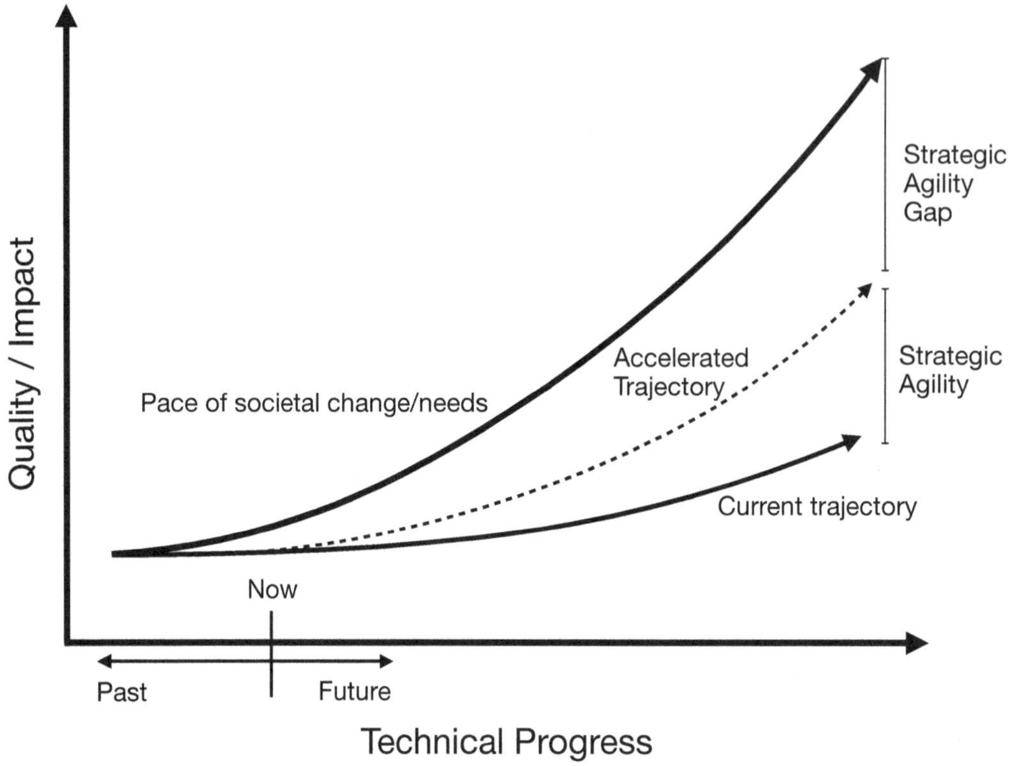

Fig. 1 The strategic agility gap

capability grows to improve performance on some criteria, interdependencies become more extensive and produce surprising anomalies as the systems also become more brittle.

The *strategic agility gap* is the difference between the rate at which an organization adapts to change and the rise of new unexpected challenges at a larger industry/society scale. It is a mismatch in velocities of change and velocities of adaptation (Fig. 1). Can organizations learn how to offset changing risks before failures occur? Can organizations build capabilities to be *poised to adapt* to keep pace with and stay ahead of the trajectory of growing complexity? The chapter addresses what drives the strategic agility gap and what adaptive capabilities organizations need to flourish in the gap.

2 Organizations in the Gap—Synchronizing Activities to Keep Pace with Cascading Events?

The gap arises as the pace of change accelerates reshaping the risks and opportunities organizations face. Organizations need the ability to adapt as challenges change. But experience shows organizations generally are slow and stale to respond to challenge events [13]. Consider high frequency computerized financial trading. Some people recognized that a relative speed advantage in trading was a special resource that could be leveraged. They invested tens of millions of dollars for slivers of relative speed, while others were oblivious to the changes underway. The speed advantage made possible through computerization led to wholly new forms of trading, such as 'dark pools', adapted to make large profits. The financial advantage of speed arose from other effects of the shift to computerized trading: expanding volumes and the multiplication of stock exchanges available. New scales of operation and speed emerged. Everything became software dependent: regulatory changes, external competitive changes, internal changes to better compete, all were changes in software. The growth trajectory resulted in new relationships, new scale of operations, new interdependencies, new tempos of operation, accompanied by new risks which were difficult to see ahead.

This trajectory of growth means disturbances/challenges can grow and cascade faster than responses can be decided on and deployed to effect. To overcome this risk requires enhancing the ability to anticipate and build a readiness-to-respond in advance of challenge events. To fail to anticipate means a new response has to be generated during the challenge event—greatly increasing the risk of failing to keep up with the tempo. This aspect of the demand trajectory in Fig. 1 means organizations need to coordinate and *synchronize activities over changing tempos, otherwise decisions will end up slow and stale.* This occurred dramatically in a case of "runaway" automation in financial trading.[1]

2.1 *Knight Capital Collapse 2012*

As one part of the organization deployed new software in order to take advantage of changes in the industry, the rollout did not go as expected, producing anomalous behavior. The team tried to rollback to the previous software configuration as is standard practice for reliability. But the rollback produced more anomalous behavior. The roles responsible for the digital infrastructure struggled to understand what produced the anomalies and why normal attempts to recover had failed. Meanwhile, automated trading continued.

It took time before the team decided to involve upper management—to say the IT team did not understand the problem, were unable to block the cascade of effects, and the only action available was to stop trading. As upper management became informed and authorized a trading stop, it was too late—automated trading had gone on so long the company was, for all practical purposes, bankrupt from an untenable market position.

[1] See https://michaelhamilton.quora.com/How-a-software-bug-made-Knight-Capital-lose-500M-in-a-day-almost-go-bankrupt and https://www.kitchensoap.com/2013/10/29/counterfactuals-knight-capital/.

The case illustrates risks for organizations in the strategic agility gap. First, small problems can interact and cascade quickly and surprisingly given the tangle of dependencies across layers inside and outside the organization. Second, as effects cascade and uncertainties grow, multiple roles struggle to understand anomalies, diagnose underlying drivers, identify compensatory actions. Third, difficulties arise getting authorization from appropriate roles to make non-routine, risky, and resource costly actions, while uncertainty remains. Fourth, all of the above take effort, time, and require coordination across roles. Meanwhile, time pressures grow as situations deteriorate. Fifth, when critical replanning decisions require serial communication vertically through the levels of the organization, responses are unable to keep pace with events. The case illustrates the need to synchronize activities across roles and layers of the organization as tempo varies.

2.2 *Coping with Hurricane Sandy 2012*

Other cases highlight how to be poised to adapt. Deary examined how a large transportation firm learned to reconfigure coordination across roles and layers when events with unpredictable risky demands occurred. He observed how the organization used these techniques during hurricane Sandy [7]. To adapt effectively, the organization:

- re-prioritized over multiple conflicting goals,
- sacrificed cost control processes in the face of safety risks,
- valued timely responsive decisions and actions,
- coordinated horizontally across functions to reduce the risk of missing critical information or side effects when replanning under time pressure,
- controlled the cost of coordination to avoid overloading already busy people and communication channels,
- pushed initiative and authority down to the lowest unit of action in the situation to increase the readiness to respond when unanticipated challenges arose.

Upper management developed mechanisms for this shift prior to particular challenge events. As hurricane Sandy approached New York, temporary teams were created quickly to provide timely updates (weather impact analysis teams). In temporary local command centers key personnel from different functions worked together to keep track of the evolving situation and re-plan. The horizontal and vertical coordination possible through these centers worked to balance the efficiency-thoroughness tradeoff in a new way for a situation that presented surprising challenges and demanded high responsiveness [10]. The firm used mechanisms to expand/speed coordination across roles in order to match the tempo of events, even though these mechanisms sacrificed economics and standard processes. These mechanisms existed because this firm's business model, environment, clientele, and external events regularly required adaptation as surprises were a normal experience.

2.3 Contrasting the Cases

The cases reveal how to be poised to adapt. Simply working to plan is not sufficient to handle exceptions, anomalies, and surprises, regardless of the contingencies built in the standard practices [14]. Anticipation and initiative are necessary in order for systems to adapt given the potential for difficulties to cascade [9]. When a unit confronts situations that challenge plans, delays are inevitable if the unit must first inform others and then wait for new instructions before initiating a response. In this reactive mode for revising plans in progress, performance is guaranteed to be slow and stale with limited ability to keep pace with change, as in the Knight Capital case. In contrast, the organization facing hurricane Sandy shifted to value responsiveness, push initiative down to units of action, and invoke mechanisms for timely coordination across roles as events unfolded.

In both cases multiple tempos of operation went on in parallel—which is basic for adaptive systems in complex worlds. When the connections across the mixed tempos were serial, responses lagged events. Facing hurricane Sandy, the other organization changed how it functioned to coordinate activities across the mix of tempos—which changed unexpectedly. From facing surprises in the past, the varying roles/levels had opportunities to exercise their coordinative 'muscles,' even though this specific event presented unique difficulties. In the strategic agility gap, the challenge for organizations is to develop new forms of coordination across functional, spatial, and temporal scales—otherwise organizations will be slow, stale and fragmented as they inevitably confront surprising challenges.

3 Systems Are Messy

The cases described to illustrate the strategic agility gap, highlight how systems are messy, fundamentally [1, 14]. All systems are developed and operate given finite resources and live in a changing environment [5]. As a result, plans, procedures, automation, all agents and roles are inherently limited and unable to completely cover the complexity of activities, events, demands, and change. All systems operate under pressures and in degraded modes. People and operations adapt to meet the inevitable challenges, pressures, trade-offs, resource scarcity, and surprises. To summarize the point vividly, Cook and Woods [6] use a coinage from the American soldier in WWII: SNAFU is the natural state of systems—where SNAFU, stands for Situation Normal All F_ _ _ ed Up. With SNAFU normal, SNAFU catching is essential—resilient performance depends on the ability to adapt outside of standard plans as these inevitably break down. SNAFU catching, however technologically facilitated, is a fundamentally human capability essential for organizational viability [15, 16]. Some people in some roles provide the essential adaptive capacity for SNAFU catching, though this may be local, underground, and invisible to distant perspectives [12].

The synthesis presented here begins with the recognition that all organizations are adaptive systems, consist of a network of adaptive systems, and exist in a web of adaptive systems—i.e., the resilience engineering paradigm. All human adaptive systems make trade-offs to cope with finite resource and all live in a changing world. The pace of change is accelerated by past successes, as growth stimulates more adaptation by more players in a more interconnected system. The scale and pace of change grow so that synchronizing over more roles at multiple tempos gets harder.

The strategic agility gap captures the dynamic whereby growing capabilities—which must produce markers of success on some indicators—also grow interdependencies and scales of operation that invoke complexity penalties (Fig. 1's mismatched trajectories). The capability growth will produce new forms of conflict, congestion, cascade and surprise so that operating in the strategic agility gap is unavoidable.

SNAFU catching is essential for the viability of adaptive systems in complex worlds. But organizations rationalize this core finding away on grounds of rarity, prevention, compliance. The first claim is: SNAFUs occur rarely given the organization's design thus investing in SNAFU catching is a narrow issue of low priority. The second claim is: there is a record of improvement that reduces the likelihood/severity/difficulty of SNAFUs. Third, when SNAFUs occur, poor response is due to people who fail to work to the rules for their role within the organization's design.

These rationalizations are wrong empirically, technically, theoretically. As organizations focus on making systems work faster, better, and cheaper, they develop new plans embodied in procedures, automation, policies, and forcing functions. These plans are seen as effective since they represent improvements relative to how the system worked previously. When surprising results occur, the organization interprets the surprises as deviations—erratic people were unable to work to plan, to work to their role within the plan, and to work to the rules prescribed for their role. The countermeasures become more stringent pressures to work-to-plan, work-to-role and work-to-rule [8]. The compliance pressure undermines the adaptive capacities needed for SNAFU catching (initiative), creates double binds that drive adaptations to make the system work 'underground,' and generates role retreat that undermines coordinated activities.

In every risky world, improvements continue, yet we also continue to experience major failures that puzzle organizations, industries, and stakeholders. SNAFU recurs visibly—in June 2018 IT failures stopped online financial trading (TSB in the UK and Canadian Stock exchanges). Befuddlement arises from a background of continued improvement on some indicators, coupled with surprising sudden performance collapses. This combination is the signature of adaptive systems in complex environments. The *scale complexity* that arises from changes to increase optimality comes at the cost of increased brittleness leading to systems

> which are robust to perturbations they were designed to handle, yet fragile to unexpected perturbations and design flaws [4, p. 2529].

As scale and interdependencies increase, a system's performance on average increases, but there is also an increase in the proportion of large collapses/failures.

Given the pursuit of optimality increases brittleness, why don't more failures occur?—SNAFU catching. Adapting to handle the regular occurrence of SNAFUs makes the work of SNAFU catching almost invisible [15]. The fluency law states:

> well adapted activity occurs with a facility that belies the difficulty of the demands resolved and the dilemmas balanced [16].

Systems that continue to adapt to changing environments, stakeholders, demands, contexts, and constraints are poised to adapt through enabling SNAFU catching [6].

Ironically, what drives the strategic agility gap is past success. Success from new capabilities produces growth. Improvements drive a pattern in adaptive cycles: effective leaders take advantage of improvements to drive systems to do more, do it faster, and in more complicated ways. Growth, and the capabilities that power it, creates opportunities for others to hijack new capabilities as they pursue their goals. Success drives increasing scale complexity which leads to the emergence of new forms of SNAFU and SNAFU catching, as systems become messy again. This is seen the rise of high frequency trading in financial markets, in ransomware, and the influence of internet bots in elections, and more. In episodes of technology change, new forms of conflict, congestion and cascade arise as apparent benefits are hijacked.

4 Continuous Adaptability

If organizations today must live in the strategic agility gap, given the growth driven by technology, how can they flourish despite complexity penalties?

Answers to this question have emerged from research on resilient performance of human adaptive systems. For organizations to flourish in the gap they need to build and sustain the ability to *continuously adapt*. Today this paradigm exists in web engineering and operations because it was necessary to keep pace with the accelerating consequences of change as new kinds of services arose from internet fueled capabilities [3]. Web-based companies live or die by the ability to scale their infrastructure to accommodate increasing demand as their services provide value. Planning for such growth requires organizations to be fluent at change and poised to adapt. Because these organizations recognize that they operate at some velocity, they know they will experience anomalies that threaten those services. Because web-based services provide growing value, the value moves from optional to standard to critical and on to existential [5].

4.1 Lessons from Web Operations

Web engineering and operations serve as a natural laboratory for studying responses to the strategic agility gap. Outages and near outages are common even at the best-in-class providers. Past success fuels the pace of change. Systems work at increasing scale in a constantly changing environment of opportunity and risk. Web engineering and operations is important also because all organizations are or are becoming digital service organizations. For example, recently multiple airlines have suffered major economic losses when IT service outages led to the collapse of the airlines ability to manage flights. Results from this natural laboratory help reveal fundamental constraints on how human adaptive systems function and how organizations can flourish in the strategic agility gap.

Organizational systems succeed despite the basic limits of plans in a complex, interdependent and changing environment because responsible people adapt to make the system work despite its design—SNAFU catching. The ingredients are:

- *anticipation*—seeing developing signs of trouble ahead to begin to adapt before the evidence is definitive (waiting till evidence is definitive almost guarantees being slow and stale);
- *contingent synchronization*—adjusting how different roles at different levels coordinate their activities to keep pace with tempo of events;
- *readiness to respond*—developing deployable and mobilizable response capabilities in advance of surprises;
- *proactive learning*—learning about brittleness and sources of resilient performance before major collapses or accidents occur by studying how surprises are caught and resolved.

4.2 Four Capabilities for Continuous Adaptation

Results on resilient performance in web operations reveals specific capabilities for effective organizations living in the gap. *Initiative* is essential for adaptation to conflicting pressures, constant risk of overload, and inevitable surprises [16]. Organizations need to guide the *expression of initiative* to ensure synchronization across roles tailored to changing situations. This requires pushing initiative down to units of action [9]. Initiative can run too wide when undirected leading to fragmentation, working at cross-purposes, and mis-synchronization across roles. However, initiative is reduced or eliminated by pressure to work-to-rule/work-to-plan, especially by threats of sanctions should adaptations prove ineffective or erroneous in hindsight. Emphasis on work-to-rule/work-to-plan compliance limits adaptive capacity when events occur that do not meet assumptions in the plan, impasses block progress, or when opportunities arise.

Resilience engineering is then left with the task of specifying what system architecture balances the expression of initiative as the potential for surprise waxes and wanes. The pressures generated by other interdependent units either energizes or reduces initiative and therefore the capacity to adapt. These pressures also change how initiative is synchronized across roles and levels. The pressures constrain and direct how the expression of initiative *prioritizes* some goals and *sacrifices* other goals when conflicts across goals intensify.

Effective organizations living in the gap build *reciprocity* across roles and levels [11]. Reciprocity in collaborative work is commitment to mutual assistance. With reciprocity, one unit donates from their limited resources now to help another in their role, so both achieve benefits for overarching goals, and trusts that when the roles are reversed, the other unit will come to its aid.

Each unit operates under limited resources in terms of energy, workload, time, attention for carrying out each role. Diverting some these resources to assist creates opportunity costs and workload management costs for the donating unit. Units can ignore other interdependent roles and focus their resources on meeting just the performance standards set for their role *alone*. Pressures for compliance undermine the willingness to reach across roles and coordinate when anomalies and surprises occur. This increases brittleness and undermines coordinated activity. Reciprocity overcomes this tendency to act selfishly and narrowly. Interdependent units in a network should show a willingness to invest energy to accommodate other units, specifically when the other units' performance is at risk.

Third, a key lesson from studies of resilience is that tangible experiences of surprise are powerful drivers for learning how to guide adaptability. Tangible experience with surprises helps organizations see SNAFU concretely and to see how people adapt as difficulties and challenges grow over time. Episodes of surprise provide the opportunity to see when and how people re-prioritize across multiple goals when operating in the midst of uncertainties, changing tempos and pressures.

Fourth, proactive learning from well-handled surprises contributes to re-calibration and model updating [15]. This starts with careful study of sets of incidents that reveal SNAFU catching [2]. What is an 'interesting' incident changes. Organizations usually reserve limited resources to study events that threatened or resulted in significant economic loss or harm to people. But this is inherently reactive and many factors narrow the learning possible. To be proactive in learning about resilience shifts the focus: study how systems work well usually despite difficulties, limited resources, trade-offs, and surprises—SNAFU catching. In addition, effective learning requires organizations to develop lightweight mechanisms to foster the spread of learning about SNAFU catching across roles and levels.

Strategic agility gap arises as organizations' trajectory of improvement cannot match the emergence of new challenges, risks, and opportunities as complexity penalties grow (Fig. 1). To flourish in the gap requires organizations to build and sustain capabilities for SNAFU catching.

References

1. D.L. Alderson, J.C. Doyle, Contrasting views of complexity and their implications for network-centric infrastructures. IEEE SMC—Part A **40**, 839–852 (2010)
2. J. Allspaw, Trade-offs under pressure: heuristics and observations of teams resolving internet service outages. Lund University, MS thesis (2015), https://lup.lub.lu.se/student-papers/search/publication/8084520

3. J. Allspaw, Human factors and ergonomics practice in web engineering and operations: navigating a critical yet opaque sea of automation, in *Human Factors and Ergonomics in Practice* ed. by S. Shorrock, C. Williams (CRC Press, Boca Raton, 2017), pp. 313–322
4. J.M. Carlson, J.C. Doyle, Highly optimized tolerance: robustness and design in complex systems. Phys. Rev. Lett. **84**(11), 2529–2532 (2000)
5. R.I. Cook, How complex systems fail, in *Velocity: Web Performance and Operations Conference*, New York (2012), https://www.youtube.com/watch?v=2S0k12uZR14
6. R.I. Cook, D.D. Woods, Situation normal: All fouled up, in *Velocity: Web Performance and Operations Conference*, New York (2016), https://www.oreilly.com/ideas/situation-normal-all-fouled-up
7. D.S. Deary, K.E. Walker, D.D. Woods, Resilience in the face of a superstorm: a transportation firm confronts hurricane sandy, in *Proceedings of the Human Factors and Ergonomics Society*, 57th Annual Meeting (Human Factors and Ergonomics Society, Santa Monica, CA, 2013), pp. 329–333. https://doi.org/10.1177/1541931213571072
8. S.W.A. Dekker, *The Safety Anarchist. Relying on Human Expertise and Innovation, Reducing Bureaucracy and Compliance* (Routledge, New York, 2018)
9. M. Finkel, *On Flexibility: Recovery from Technological and Doctrinal Surprise on the Battlefield* (Stanford Security Studies, Palo Alto, 2011)
10. E. Hollnagel, *The ETTO principle: efficiency-thoroughness trade-off: why things that go right sometimes go wrong* (Ashgate, Farnham, 2009)
11. E. Ostrom, Toward a Behavioral Theory Linking Trust, Reciprocity, and Reputation, in *Trust and Reciprocity: Interdisciplinary Lessons from Experimental Research*, ed. by E. Ostrom, J. Walker (Russell Sage Foundation, NY, 2003)
12. S. Perry, R. Wears, Underground adaptations: cases from health care. Cogn. Technol. Work **14**, 253–260 (2012). https://doi.org/10.1007/s10111-011-0207-2
13. D.D. Woods, M. Branlat, How Adaptive Systems Fail, in *Resilience Engineering in Practice*, ed. by E. Hollnagel, J. Paries, D.D. Woods, J. Wreathall (Ashgate, Aldershot, 2011), pp. 127–143
14. D.D. Woods, Four concepts of resilience and the implications for resilience engineering. Reliab. Eng. Syst. Saf. **141**, 5–9 (2015). https://doi.org/10.1016/j.ress.2015.03.018
15. D.D. Woods (ed.), STELLA report from the SNAFUcatchers workshop on coping with complexity. SNAFU Catchers Consortium, downloaded from stella.report. Accessed 10 April 2017
16. D.D. Woods, The theory of graceful extensibility. Environ. Syst. Decis. **38**, 433–457 (2018). https://doi.org/10.1007/s10669-018-9708-3

The Languages of Safety

Hervé Laroche

Abstract Human and organizational factors (HOF) specialists have worked hard to develop a body of methods, tools, concepts, etc., that allow them to fulfil their mission in a professional way within their companies. Yet they are often frustrated and feel that they do not get the attention they deserve. Several of the chapters of the present volume can be read as invitations for HOF specialists to develop a different approach and adopt new types of discourse in order to get more attention from managers. I review four possible "languages" and discuss how and to what extent they would give more power to HOF specialists. I conclude by inviting safety people to use a variety of languages for a variety of audiences.

Keywords Attention · Manager · HOF specialists · Discourse

1 Introduction

It's a fact: managers are not naturally excited by human and organizational factors (HOF) issues. Yes, top managers are always ready to issue strong verbal commitments to safety and to set zero accident objectives. However, when it comes to budgeting HOF actions, hiring specialists, launching studies and projects, managers appear less convinced of the safety imperatives and show limited faith in the contribution of HOF methods and people. HOF specialists have to find a way of getting managers' attention in times when no accidents are happening. How can they do that? In this book, four different answers are given to this question:

- Talk hard science (Paul Schulman, Chap. 9),
- Talk numbers and money (Daniel Mauriño, Chap. 10),
- Talk law and blame (Caroline Lacroix, Chap. 8),
- Talk complexity (David Woods, Chap. 11).

H. Laroche (✉)
ESCP Europe, Paris, France
e-mail: laroche@escpeurope.eu

B. Journé et al. (eds.), *Human and Organisational Factors*,
SpringerBriefs in Safety Management,
https://doi.org/10.1007/978-3-030-25639-5_12

I will now discuss each of them, not so much on the grounds of the ideas themselves, rather on the basis of their relevance for getting attention from managers.

2 Talk Hard Science

Paul Schulman's assessment of the social sciences contribution to safety is rather grim. Social scientists failed to get the ear of engineers who (rightly, according to Schulman) find their concepts underspecified and their methods dubious. In short, they have done bad science. Fortunately, social scientists can still amend themselves by imitating the practices of the engineering sciences, using clearly defined variables and building rigorous metrics.

There is no doubt that this view of scientific excellence would make many social scientists very angry. Leaving this aside, would the alignment of HOF science methods with engineering science methods make the possible contributions from HOF more attractive in the eyes of managers? This could be the case, if managers have training in engineering, which is not uncommon in many industries. Yet, the sociology of the managerial elites has evolved and is still evolving in a direction that does not favor the engineering culture. Engineers and people from the trades have lost precedence over professional managers (MBAs), finance-oriented people, and more or less self-made entrepreneurs. It is also unlikely that hardened HOF science could compete with the faith in algorithmic power of the GAFA-type firms.

Adverse effects can happen. Managers certainly have little respect for the social sciences, compared with the engineering sciences. Yet they are keen on the psychological aspects, like leadership, soft skills, meditation and mindfulness, etc. They often become obsessed with these dubious concepts, making "serious" social scientists and people inspired by the social sciences despair. Talking hard science will not protect them from these fads. Indeed, it is more likely than they will fall for it more easily, meaning not-so-good social science will be replaced by quite worse pseudo-social science.

3 Talk Numbers and Money

Daniel Mauriño takes an opposite view to Schulman's. For him, safety specialists are already too grounded in engineering science. Rather than talking like engineers to impress managers, he advocates, safety specialists should talk like managers. Safety should become a business function just like any other and talk the same language (allocation of resources, budgets, contribution to performance, etc.). In short, if HOF experts turn themselves into managers, the other managers will listen to them.

This reminds me of the famous words pronounced during the meeting the night before the Challenger launch in 1986 [2]. After two hours of discussion about the impact of low temperatures on the O'rings, the head of Engineering from Morton

Thiokol was urged by his boss to *"put down his engineering hat and put on his management hat"*. Behind these words we find a myth: engineers are supposed to aim at perfection and worry only about technology while managers are supposed to seek operational performance and worry about money. Everybody is happy with this myth. Managers gain the power of making the final decisions while engineers keep their hands clean. In the Challenger meeting, the engineers did not contest the final decision made by managers, though many were still convinced that it was "away from goodness". What Daniel Mauriño proposes is that safety people, and especially HOF people put on a management hat and get their hands dirty. This is the only way to gain more power and to do their job properly.

Just as Schulman's conception of scientific rigour can be questioned, Mauriño's understanding of what management means is debatable. For Mauriño, management is direction, supervision and control. Basically, this is what Henri Fayol proposed as early as 1916 in his *Administration Industrielle et Générale* [1]. A problem is that Fayol-type definitions of management are very abstract and have little use when it comes to describing what managers really do and how organizations really work. Organization theories provide a much more complex portrait of what constitutes an organization and these theories suggest that establishing safety as a function does not guarantee that it will have more influence. What happens when safety specialists behave like managers? Maybe they get the ear of other managers, but what will they tell them? In advocating for safety specialists to renounce their obsession with accident prevention, Mauriño demonstrates his faith in the rationality of management. Reasonable (that is, calculated) decisions will be made by well-informed managers. What the Challenger case suggests is that unreasonable choices can be made by managers AND engineers, not because they are evil but because they lose sight of what they are really doing and of the consequences of their choices (hence the famous concept of normalization of deviance [2]).

As Mauriño frames it, safety specialists face a strategic choice: either they change their identity and their language to become "safety financial officers", as Mauriño suggests, or they remain an independent, accident-obsessed safety service, trying to give more weight to the avoidance of accidents. But this means, in fact, giving more weight to the fear of accidents and their consequences; in short, scaring managers.

4 Talk Law and Blame

According to Caroline Lacroix, managers should be scared already: there is a clear trend towards an increasing intervention of judges in verifying the compliance of some companies (judicialization) and towards the intervention of the criminal justice system when accidents happen (criminalization).

It is unclear, though, to what extent these trends have negative consequences for companies (direct or indirect costs) and managers (convictions, loss of position, etc.). Being brought before a criminal court of justice is certainly a frightening prospect for a manager. Yet big companies and top executives benefit from powerful legal counsel. Criminalization of safety issues could just result in an escalation of legal disputes. Indeed, ultimately, the level of deterrence may not be significantly increased, at least not enough to have an effect on the behaviour of firms and of managers. In fact, although there is a shortage of systematic data, the impression one gets from recent cases is that, whatever the costs, big companies can survive any kind of accident unless they are already economically or politically in a very weak condition. The criminalization of safety issues might even offer some latitude to powerful organizations, in that criminal justice is often very slow and offers many opportunities for delaying tactics. A financially robust organization can easily gain time and buffer the shock of the accident. Besides, once an accident has happened, nobody has a real interest in weakening the company. Workers want to keep their jobs and victims want to be compensated.

Let us suppose, though, that these trends in the world of law and justice have some deterrence potential. Should safety specialists try and take advantage of that? Such a strategy would imply that safety specialists strengthen their abilities in legal matters, or that they make an alliance with legal experts. Both are unlikely. Investment in legal competencies is very costly. And legal experts, who enjoy the privilege of direct access to top executives, have no interest in opening their jurisdiction to safety specialists. As noted by Caroline Lacroix, safety specialists might even have much to lose. A logical consequence of increased criminalization is the reinforcement of a "blame culture" down the entire managerial line. Safety specialists who have relentlessly worked at promoting a "just culture" based on the contribution of the HOF science would be shooting themselves in the foot.

For safety specialists, talking law and blame is thus not an option, though they may gain some influence if, as Lacroix suggests, the courts become more knowledgeable about safety science, and more specifically about HOF science. In highly regulated industries, where dialogue with the regulatory bodies has an anticipatory orientation and goes deeper into the technicalities of the safety issues, there is perhaps more hope. Sitting at the boundary of the regulatory environment is certainly a source of influence for safety specialists. Up to what point is, however, debatable.

5 Talk Complexity and Change

All the ways of gaining influence examined previously are based on attempts to adopt a simple, rational language. Engineering science may be highly technical, yet fundamentally it is just analytic knowledge. The language of safety as a business function is also based on a rational view of an organization, which can be broken down into smaller parts (functions). Law, however esoteric it may appear to the eyes of the lay person, is after all, as Weber told us, the instrument of reason in the social world. Engineering science, management practices and legal knowledge have relied on analytic knowledge to bring stability and control.

David Woods comes up with a quite different view. His core idea is that analytic simplification is an obsolete way of gaining control of today's sociotechnical systems.

Sociotechnical systems have changed in nature, he contends. The key metaphor is no longer the chemical plant or the nuclear power station or a transportation system. Rather, it is the computerized, algorithmic, decentralized, connected, highly autonomous, evolving system. With these systems, do not expect stability, expect change and evolution. You will always be late and you will never achieve full control: there will always be glitches, small ones and big ones (which he calls SNAFU[1]s). Catch them before they kill you. We are in a world of complexity.

As with the other contributions, I will not discuss his ideas per se, but will rather examine their potential power for allowing safety specialists to gain influence. In this respect, his metaphor of complexity has two very strong features. Firstly, it is in line with the "third industrial revolution" that everyone sees unfolding in all industries and in our daily life. Secondly, it gives us a future. The fourth and fifth industrial revolutions are on their way. I am not making predictions: I am talking about what is on people's minds today. There is little doubt that managers will love that, if only because their biggest fear is to be seen as outdated. Symbolically, they now compete with Elon Musk, Jeff Bezos or the people from Google. Besides, the complexity paradigm gives them an opportunity to master a discourse with a potential for managerial autonomy and legitimacy, after decades of finance-oriented, shareholder domination. The complexity paradigm gives power to insiders because the key knowledge will be held and operated by them and will remain, to a large extent, opaque to external stakeholders.

I see no reason why safety specialists could not embrace the complexity paradigm. Complexity is compatible with HOF, on the overall. For instance, no major effort is needed to insert into it HRO[2] concepts or the views of Karl Weick. This does not mean that HOF specialists should always bow to the discourse of the complexity gurus, only that they should find their voice and contribute. In its present versions the complexity paradigm might well seem to forget the HOFs, but this is only one more reason to connect with it.

6 Final Comments

Safety and HOFs need to be "sexed up". HOF specialists are people in the trade that are equipped to talk to other people in the trade, not to a class of managers that have a universal view of their jobs and careers. These managers are more likely to embrace the complexity paradigm than traditional engineering or standard managerial thinking. Complexity is however a vast territory and there is no reason why HOF specialists could not find their place in it.

Yet, rather than being obsessed with the top management, safety specialists should also work at building a network of influence at all levels in the organizations. Managers are a target that can be reached directly or indirectly and talking numbers and

[1]Situation Normal All F_ _ _ ed Up.

[2]High reliability organizations.

money is a direct way of influence. There is no doubt that safety specialists could make progress in this respect. Talking hard science can help them get the ears of engineers, and engineers can relay their inputs to managers. Undoubtedly, talking law cannot hurt, although there is little opportunity for direct power, except in the institutional work of building external networks of expertise (setting standards, etc.).

My suggestion is that safety people learn and practice several languages for different audiences. I do not think they have to worry too much about possible contradictions. Local and provisional coherence is what matters in organizations. Global and continuous coherence is only a question of identity. Safety people do not need a specific language to foster their identity. They have better than that: they have a mission.

References

1. H. Fayol, Administration Industrielle et Générale. Bull. Société de l'Industrie Minérale **10**, 5–164 (1916)
2. D. Vaughan, *The Challenger Launch Decision* (University of Chicago Press, 1996)

The Dual Face of HOF in High-Risk Organizations

Corinne Bieder

Abstract High-risk organizations commonly acknowledge the importance of human and organizational factors (HOF). However, in practice the role played by HOF specialists and their share of voice varies dramatically from one organization to another. Within organizations themselves, there are some recurrent tensions around HOF and the role HOF specialists are understood to play. This delicate situation seems to partly stem from the gap between conventional wisdom on HOF in high-risk organizations and how HOF specialists see HOF and their role and contribution to organizations. Exploring this dual face of HOF and trying to better understand where it comes from may help to reduce misunderstandings and suggest ways forward to build on the remaining inevitable organizational contradictions to improve the way HOF are considered in high-risk industries.

Keywords Human factors · Organizational factors · Safety · Complexity

1 Introduction

Although the importance of human and organizational factors (HOF) for safety is widely and commonly acknowledged in high-risk organizations, the reality is more qualified as to how this 'importance' translates into practice. Drawing a general picture that would pretend to be representative of all high-risk organizations or even of all parts of a given organization would be oversimplifying a diverse reality. In addition, the way HOF are taken into account varies in time, along with the context, the people and probably many other factors that would be worth exploring. However, in some parts of some organizations, as the issues raised by FonCSI's industrial partners go to show, there is a recurrent emergence of tensions around HOF and the role HOF specialists are understood to play. These tensions seem to partly stem from the gap between conventional wisdom on HOF in high-risk organizations and how HOF specialists see HOF and their role and contribution to organizations. Exploring

C. Bieder (✉)
ENAC, University of Toulouse, Toulouse, France
e-mail: corinne.bieder@enac.fr

B. Journé et al. (eds.), *Human and Organisational Factors*,
SpringerBriefs in Safety Management,
https://doi.org/10.1007/978-3-030-25639-5_13

the gap between this dual face of HOF and trying to characterize it may be a starting point for envisaging ways forward to improve the way HOF are considered in high-risk industries.

2 How HOF Specialists See HOF and How They See their Role

Human and organizational factors are understood in many different ways, including among so-called HOF specialists depending on their earlier education, background, experience… The emphasis may vary from one HOF specialist to another (e.g. individual or organizational mechanisms, psychological, ergonomics or more social aspects). However, it is commonly agreed that overall, HOF are both a specific body of scientific knowledge on a range of aspects such as human cognition, physiology, organizational mechanisms and a set of scientific methodologies to apprehend real work situations. This distinction between what is at play in real work situations and a theoretical view of how work should be done or how organizations should function is at the core of HOF.

This specific scientific and methodological background leads HOF specialists to consider themselves as experts. Indeed, this knowledge is not commonly passed on in educational or training paths other than the social sciences. In a sense, HOF specialists see their role as the experts of reality, the spokespersons for the distinction between real practices and theoretical processes and procedures, between organizational charts and organizations considered as living 'bodies'. In other words, they see their role as the constant reality bell in managers and decision-makers minds. By bringing reality to the surface, although it is reality seen through the lenses of their conceptual, theoretical and methodological background, they see their role as the voice of reality, the one that everyone should absolutely listen to and consider, at all levels of the organization including the highest echelons, to acknowledge these differences and take benefits from them to enhance safety and more generally to improve the overall performance.

Even though HOF specialists may initially intervene to enhance safety, analyzing how work is done in reality and how organizations actually function goes beyond the sole safety dimension. In this respect, they see their scope as broader than just safety, encompassing all aspects of the way the organization functions and is managed.

Thus, they see their positioning as a core part of business management to improve not only safety but the global performance of an organization, even if in high-risk domains, safety is a key dimension of the global performance. However, such positioning may appear to some extent in contradiction with the claim of expert knowledge. Indeed, as characterized by Ardoino [1], the expert is called upon to solve a problem with limited scope for which the expert is known to have high levels of knowledge and competence. In contrast, the positioning of HOF specialists would correspond to that of consultant [1] (or process facilitator as called by Schein [5]), meaning they intervene with the aim of modifying or changing representations, attitudes and the like through longer interventions and joint work with the 'client', including on the problem statement and request.

Ironically, although HOF specialists claim to be experts in how reality works, how HOF specialists see themselves could be considered a description of how HOF specialists *should* be seen, rather than how they are seen in reality. Indeed, decision-makers and top managers seem to have different views on HOF and the role of HOF specialists in high-risk organizations, at least according to what HOF specialists perceive.

3 How Decision Makers and Top Management See HOF and the Role of HOF Specialists

One of the reasons for the gap between how HOF specialists see their role and how managers see it lies in their different views on HOF. If HOF specialists see the reality of work through their social science lenses, managers, whatever their level, see reality through their managerial body of knowledge and tools lenses. Again, generalizing how managers see HOF is too simplistic and caricatural an approach, but it helps to point out where some of the current difficulties, misunderstandings and frustrations come from, and to envisage possible ways forward. Conventional wisdom on HOF in high-risk industries assumes, among others, that there can be a good organization (understood as organizational structure), that everything can be described and prescribed in processes and procedures, and that if everybody complies with these requirements, it is the best way to ensure safety [3]. Indeed, this is how quality is ensured.

With this understanding of HOF in mind, HOF specialists are seen as experts having established knowledge on a limited defined scope [1, 5], human and organizational aspects, able to help solving problems with the organizational structure or processes or procedures, through quick interventions aiming at improving them or providing knowledge/data to improve them. They can act as a support to the implementation of the current management model through inputs to improve or develop operational processes and procedures, sometimes even organizational structural settings that are obviously directly related to safety.

Another aspect of their role is to serve as an 'alibi' for external justification. By having identified HOF specialists, the organization can claim it takes HOF into account, whatever their actual role and influence.

Regarding their primary role, their scope is naturally limited to the improvement or further development of how HOF are seen (i.e. good procedures, processes, organizational structure, selection, training…) in order to enhance safety.

Their positioning is therefore a side function supporting business which is the core function as it is meant, taught, thought in business training (i.e. mainly production and efficiency).

Whereas the ambition of HOF specialists could be understood as revolutionary with regard to how organizations are run and managed, what managers expect from HOF specialists is far more modest and limited in scope. It comes down to providing support to improve their current safety management practices, which means actionable recommendations to improve prescriptions, which HOF specialists are most often reluctant to formulate. Indeed, HOF specialists consider, with their viewpoint strongly anchored in the reality of work, that prescriptions cannot be developed exclusively top-down. Instead, they claim that the operators themselves, the ones who have the best field expertise and who will be using the prescriptions, should be involved in their development.

Eventually, significant tensions exist around how the role of HOF specialists is perceived by HOF specialists themselves and managers respectively. To take an engineering metaphor, from the point of view of managers, HOF specialists should focus on the refinement of the human-machine interface rather than on the definition of the functionalities of a technical system. To take another metaphor, they should be good at reporting minor facts of the world, like Clark Kent does, rather than trying to save the world as Superman does. Yet, functionality and interface both influence each other and also ultimately what a socio-technical system will do and how it will perform… Just as Clark Kent is part of Superman and Superman is part of Clark Kent….

4 How to Make these Tensions Constructive: Reconciling Superman and Clark Kent?

Is there a constructive way forward to handle this significant gap between the two faces of HOF? Would it make sense to try and turn Superman into Clark Kent or conversely, to try and turn Clark Kent into Superman? Would the world be better if these two faces became a single one?

Coming back to the (at least) dual face of HOF, shedding light on these questions would definitely require further investigation and refinement in several areas. As mentioned earlier, a first area would be to get away from a single homogeneous category when referring to HOF as well as to HOF specialists. The way they perceive themselves as well as the way they believe they are perceived may be significantly diverse. Likewise, managers are not a single homogeneous lot and would deserve a refined categorization. Their understanding of HOF and of the role of HOF specialists may vary dramatically with a number of factors to be investigated.

Nevertheless, HOF can be characterized as a specific way to look at work and organizations (a more realistic one would claim HOF specialists). In a sense, HOF can be seen as a way to make progress in ignorance by bringing to the surface and recognizing uncertainty and contradictions in real work situations, where the dominating management models often tend to seek to eliminate uncertainty and contradictions. If, currently, both are seen as competing with one another and trying to impose their respective view, leading to frustration, could other ways forward be explored?

Integration of HOF into engineering models, business models, etc., is often suggested (see Laroche, chapter "The Languages of Safety", this volume). Yet, integration leads to giving up the diversity of views and approaches, and ultimately leads to holism rather than reflecting the complexity of reality. Yet, it is precisely this complexity of reality that HOF specialists try hard to advocate in their daily work by highlighting the interrelations between individuals and/or organizational entities, how they organize themselves as well as the antagonistic objectives and characteristics at play. In this respect, integrating HOF into other dimensions, and contenting oneself with it, would be selling HOF's soul to the devil. As would be trying to impose HOF views on the overall way the organization is managed, thereby killing the requisite variety. Acknowledging contradictions, complexity, uncertainties, in a sense the need for system thinking, is part of HOF experience, if not at the core of it, and not trying to eliminate all of the competitive and antagonistic characteristics between the parts is precisely at the core of system thinking [4].

More exchanges between HOF specialists and managers, developing a better understanding of their respective worlds and views could possibly help to resolve unnecessary contradictions (not all contradictions) and could be a middle way to explore between the integration and missionary extremes. For a start, it would help to adjust the type of interventions and postures of HOF specialists to the context and conditions, between content expert, process facilitator [5] or a more political action through generic "speech" and models with a performative aim to change representations on the role of humans and organizations in safety [2].

Nevertheless, the inevitable remaining contradictions will perpetrate, at least to some extent, the dual face of HOF and its ambivalent effect. HOF specialists will continue to propose ways forward, although they know there is no definite and sustainable solution despite what managers believe and expect. They will thereby continue to create disappointment and frustration at the manager level, but at the same time, will continue to claim they were not given sufficient leeway to act and that more interventions are needed. A tricky simultaneously vicious and virtuous circle!

References

1. J. Ardoino, Les postures (ou impostures) respectives du chercheur, de l'expert et du consultant. Les nouvelles formes de la recherche en éducation **2**, 79–87 (1990)
2. P. Bourdieu, *Décrire et prescrire [Note sur les conditions de possibilité et les limites de l'efficacité politique]*, in *Actes de la recherche en sciences sociales*, vol. 38, mai 1981. La représentation politique-2 (1981), pp. 69–73. https://doi.org/10.3406/arss.1981.2120, https://www.persee.fr/doc/arss_0335-5322_1981_num_38_1_2120
3. IRSN, Les Facteurs Organisationnels et Humains de la gestion des risques: idées reçues, idées déçues. Rapport DSR n°438 (2011)

4. E. Morin, From the concept of system to the paradigm of complexity. J. Soc. Evol. Syst. **15**(4), 371–385 (1992)
5. E.H. Schein, The role of the consultant: content expert or process facilitator? J. Couns. Dev. **56**(6), 339–343 (1978)

Human and Organisational Factors: Fad or not Fad?

Jean-Christophe Le Coze

Abstract In this chapter, I take a step back in order to add some elements of discussion by embedding human and organisational factors within a broader historical and sociological context that has so far not been available in the literature. The reason for doing so is that there is a proliferation of various methods, ideas and models in this area. By comparing this phenomenon with the development, over the past two to three decades, of a management market in which consulting companies, business schools and publishers constitute the main actors and institutions, it is shown that human and organisational factors can also be described through similar patterns. I conclude the chapter with a suggestion that one important task for industries and regulators might be to help clarify expectations considering this diversity.

Keywords Human and organisational factors · Fads · Safety products and market · Consulting · Research · Regulators

1 Introduction

In the past 20 years in France and in other countries, the expression "human and organisational factors" (HOF) has become the standard way to refer to a wide range of contributions in the field of safety. These contributions rely on the human and social sciences to assert the importance of properly addressing the specific characteristics of humans and organisations in sociotechnical systems, a problem amplified in safety critical or high-risk systems (nuclear power plants, aircrafts, chemical plants, railways, etc.) due to their hazardous potential. A wide range of disciplines are involved, including psychology, social-psychology, ergonomics, management and sociology.

In the field of safety, this expression, HOF, very often embraces a continuum or perhaps, what could be best described as a mixture of research and practice, of academics and consultants, of regulators and actors of private companies all of whom are involved in the production, promotion and conceptualisation of methods, ideas

J.-C. Le Coze (✉)
INERIS, Verneuil-en-Halatte, France
e-mail: Jean-Christophe.LECOZE@ineris.fr

B. Journé et al. (eds.), *Human and Organisational Factors*,
SpringerBriefs in Safety Management,
https://doi.org/10.1007/978-3-030-25639-5_14

and models. Safety culture, crew resource management, behavioural based safety, high-reliability organisations, swiss cheese, just culture, safety check-list, safety leadership, golden rules, vision zero, resilience engineering or safety II…are the most visible examples [14].

This proliferation of ideas, methods, practices and models has never really been studied although it is an intriguing phenomenon.

Yet, the development of human and organisational factors is parallel to a similar but even broader dynamic in the past 20–30 years which has been empirically studied by management researchers, namely the explosion of a market for management ideas in the 1980s, served by a thriving consulting industry [3–5, 11, 15, 16]. Researchers of this topic are interested in different aspects of its evolution, and their work provides highly relevant insights to thinking about human and organisational factors.

2 Studying Management as a Market

The knowledge economy, the post-industrial, information or network society are examples of expressions designed to capture some of the macro-mutations of the past decades in areas of work, organisations or capitalism in which the service economy has a central place, including consulting. In this discourse, knowledge is at the heart of the competitive advantage of companies, and managerial innovation is part of this trend, supported by a diversity of actors.

Authors writing about management consulting adopt a variety of angles ranging from historical, psychological, economic to sociological lenses. Topics include, for instance, the origin and history of management consulting, the issue of fads and fashions in management methods, the rise of management gurus, the structure of consulting companies, the identity of consultants or the client-consultant relationship. They illustrate and explain how management, over the last two decades, has evolved into a highly dynamic market, where companies consume management products available in many forms. These can be books, conferences, videos or services by consultants. Let us comment briefly on a selected number of these topics.

The increased number, size and complexity of corporations, the presence of the military industrial complex, the development of many administrations but also the expansion of business schools and business press constitute the historical background driving this explosion during the second half of the 20th Century. In a nutshell, the advent of a new class of employees differentiated from company owners at the beginning of the 20th Century, namely managers, combined with the increasing size and complexity of corporations, produced a need for education in the new area of management. Business schools were created out of this need, and research in management followed, feeding a scientific, business and management press publishing periodicals, journals and books on the topic.

The institutional view of this phenomenon, conceptualising the interactions between business schools, private consulting companies and business publishers and press, pursues this historical analysis into our present situation to show how these key actors generate and fuel the dynamic of the past two to three decades in this area [5, 15].

Part of this dynamic of the management market has been described as having the traits of management fashions or fads [10]. Researchers have identified cycles that resemble fashion but applied to management, namely a rise and fall of methods, ideas, tools or practices which companies apply in sequence, or sometimes in combination, but which change as time passes. Well-known examples abound. Total quality management, corporate culture, balanced scoreboard, business re-engineering, leadership, six sigma, lean management, empowerment or digital disruption are some of these cases of very popular themes that anyone with working experience is bound to have heard of.

Hypothesised reasons for such cycles of fashions or fads are numerous. They range from the quality of how well these products are marketed to be appealing to consumers, to the insecurity of managers. They thus offer simple principles to deal with a still-complex management problem. They bring elements of response to the need to feel in control, and they also support the construction of a management identity by framing expectations. In addition, they are sufficiently flexible to be applied in various contexts which makes them quite unspecified and not restricted to a particular area. After a while, once a product has been sold successfully, new offers emerge which capture another way of improving management, based on alternative principles to those of the current fashion. And the cycle continues.

Now, these fashions and fads do not operate in a simplistic way, and one criticism of some of these studies is their absence of empirical analysis about the way managers and employees of corporations actually use these methods and ideas. This area, referred to as the client-consultant relationship, has various analytical facets, from critical to more neutral ones. The critical view by academics sees in these trends a capitalist drive for making profits and for ideologically influencing the way managers think about how they see people, businesses and markets.

They see consultants exploiting the need of managers to be reassured, to be helped with simplistic ideas, to impress others through cutting-edge thinking, etc. One problem is that they also tend to simplify the reality of how methods and ideas really travel from consultant to management and employees of organisations in practice, but also how new management ideas are produced. Let us comment on these two aspects. First, people in organisations are not passive recipients of management recipes. They can be highly suspicious (or even cynical) and are, at least, systematically active translators of these methods and ideas. Of course, to talk of people in organisations in general is not good enough, because it is important to distinguish categories of people here; between the diversity of hierarchical and functional layers of organisations, there are as many views as there are individuals.

For instance, it is not unusual for top management to embrace new managerial fashions when lower levels of the organisation are unimpressed by them, sometimes reluctant to deploy the fad or even resisting its implementation, whether promoted or not with the help of consultants. But the competition between consultants is also fierce, all of them competing to get the attention of their potential buyers and consumers of services. Consultants in their diversity are in very different positions with companies, and also struggle to sell their products and expertise, depending on complex decision-making processes within organisations, between the presentations of their ideas to obtaining a contract [17].

The relationship between consultants, ideas, methods and real practices is therefore more complex than the critical, or one-way, approach suggests. People in organisations are never totally passive consumers of management products, but are active translators instead. In relation to this, and as the second point, methods and ideas advocated by consultants do not come out of nowhere…they are in many cases coming from the practices of individuals in companies that innovate. These people innovate but without necessarily conceptualising their practices then marketing and selling them; but consultants do. So, again, the relationship between organisations, consultants, methods and ideas is far more complex than a one-way vision.

3 Human and Organisational Factors in the Light of Management Market Research

This summarised picture of some of the research topics and outcomes associated with the study of the management market should be familiar to anyone involved in safety research and practice because the patterns described and analysed above correspond, at least partly, to what has happened in this field over the past two to three decades. Similarly, as introduced briefly earlier, an explosion of methods, ideas and consultants has been seen. In 1988, only a few human and organisational methods or concepts were available in comparison to the situation thirty years later in 2018.

The concept of safety culture did not really exist at the time, or was only starting to be mentioned explicitly. The practice of crew resource management was in its infancy. The notion of human error was only ten years old, with major conceptualisation still to come. High reliability organisation was not a management label and was only a recently published idea. So, it is mainly in the past two to three decades, like with management, that the explosion of a safety market has occurred.

It is very tempting to copy and paste the mode of institutional analysis applied in management research, from a historical and sociological point of view. Comparable actors and institutions are involved in the production of a safety market: consultants, academics, safety publishers and press. There are no quantitative figures which would help to substantiate a comparison between the two fields, management and safety. One can imagine without taking too much risk that the safety market is only a tiny fraction of what the management market represents but the analogy between the two is still highly informative.

One major difference is the importance and presence of active regulators. In safety, and more so in high-risk systems, regulators can be the promoters of certain methods and ideas, and cases of prescribed notions such as just culture, safety culture or resilience are now available. In concrete terms, this means that such concepts have become expected and required in various contexts through regulations. Therefore,

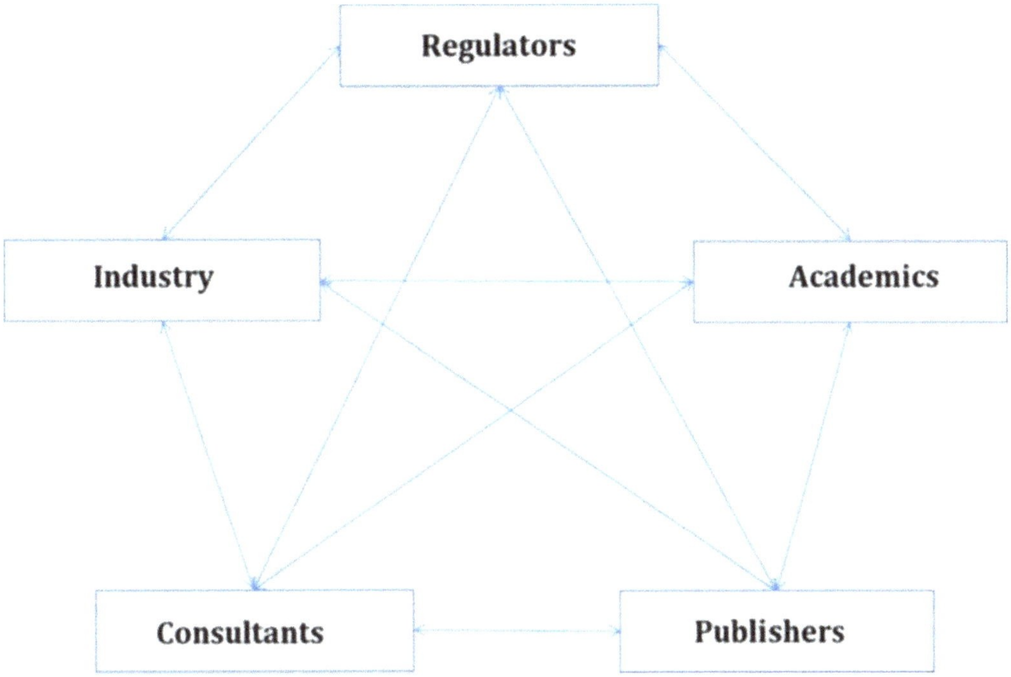

Fig. 1 Core actors and institutions of the safety market

one needs to slightly expand the key actors and institutions behind the safety market in comparison with the management market, to include the regulators (Fig. 1).

One message of this chapter is that to understand human and organisational factors, one also therefore needs to understand the complex paths followed by concepts as products of the interactions between these different actors and institutions, following and extending Laroche's commodification approach of safety culture [12]. The methods and ideas of human and organisational factors have different historical and sociological trajectories. Let us illustrate these briefly with one example, safety culture [14].

The story of safety culture (SC) can be found in many articles and books [2]. Its origin is linked to Chernobyl and some official reports referring to this idea. From there, the concept was picked up in several directions, some more academically oriented, some more practically oriented. From the academic point of view, it is a controversial notion [1], with opposing views about its value, from scholars who produce practical versions to be implemented by multinationals (e.g. [8]) to those who reject it (e.g. [7]). Safety culture is a fairly well-established product sold by consultants when associated with the maturity principle which sets out that there are several stages of achievement [6]. And safety culture has also been introduced into regulations, such as in the Norwegian petroleum industry (for a recent discussion, see Antonsen et al. [2].

Other cases of methods, ideas, models and concepts exist (e.g. crew resource management, behavioural based safety, high reliability organisations, vision zero, just culture, resilience, etc., see [13]. They would reveal the complexity of the interactions between the different actors generating them, and the patterns associated.

4 Discussion and Conclusion

This proliferation of available methods, ideas, models and consultants gives rise to many questions if one pursues the comparison with the management market studies, and if one considers that companies internalise as much as externalise their human and organisational factors expertise (see the case of UK railway in Ryan, this book, chapter "Accounting for Differing Perspectives and Values: The Rail Industry"). One is about fashions and fads. *Can we consider the abundance of products in human and organisational factors to be fashions or fads? Are human and organisational factors different? If yes, why and how?* A follow-up question could be *How do organisations deal with this diversity of products, whether fads or not fads? How do companies articulate this diversity? Do they? Does it differ between high-risk industries considering their diverse contexts?* Another one is about practices. *How are these safety products concretely translated in organisational practices? How do they efficiently contribute to create, improve or maintain safety?*

More work is needed if one considers these to be important questions. They are clearly quite complex ones requiring empirical investigations, but it seems obvious that facing this diversity of possibilities, companies are, for the moment, left to think for themselves about the best options to follow, and some chapters of this book illustrate this with concrete examples. Maturity in this respect depends on the resources and context of high-risk systems, aviation probably being at the high-end (Reuzeau, this book, chapter "The Key Drivers to Setting up a Valuable and Sustainable HOF Approach in a High-Risk Company such as Airbus") while other industries at a lower end of the continuum.

If regulators are important actors and institutions promoting the introduction of human and organisational factors (Mearns, this book, chapter "Safety Leadership and Human and Organisational Factors (HOF)—Where Do We Go from Here?"), then one role they could play, with the support of academics, consultants and industry experts, is to offer guidance about what is expected from high-risk systems in terms of the different possibilities available offered to improve practices with the help of this diversity of methods, ideas and models. This would not imply going as far as prescribing the use of particular methods but providing clarity instead among their diversity (e.g. [9]).

References

1. S. Antonsen, Safety culture assessment: a mission impossible? J. Contingencies Crisis Manag. **17**(4), 242–254 (2009)
2. S. Antonsen, M. Nilsen, P. Almklov, Regulating the intangible. Searching for safety culture in the Norwegian petroleum industry. Saf. Sci. **92**, 232–240 (2017)
3. T. Clark, R. Fincham, *Critical Consulting: New Perspectives on the Management Advice Industry* (Blackwell, Oxford, 2002)
4. T. Clark, M. Kipping, *The Oxford Handbook of Management Consulting* (Oxford University Press, Oxford, 2012)

5. L. Engwall, M. Kipping, B. Üsdiken, *Defining Management. Business Schools, Consultants, Media* (Routledge, New York, 2016)
6. A.P. Goncalves Filho, P. Waterson, Maturity models and safety culture: a critical review. Saf. Sci. **105**, 192–211 (2018)
7. A. Hopkins, Quiet outrage. The way of a sociologist (2016). Wolters Kluwer CCH
8. P. Hudson, Implementing a safety culture in a major multi-national. Saf. Sci. **45**, 697–722 (2007)
9. INERIS, Guide Ingénierie FOH (2018), www.ineris.fr
10. N. Jung, A. Kieser, Consultants in the management fashion arena, in *The Oxford Handbook of Management Consulting*, ed. by T. Clark, M. Kipping (Oxford University Press, Oxford, 2012), pp. 327–346
11. M. Kipping, L. Engwall, *Management consulting. Emergence and dynamics of a knowledge industry* (Oxford University Press, Oxford, 2002)
12. H. Laroche, The commodification of safety culture and how to escape it, in *Safety Cultures, Safety Models: Taking Stock and Moving Forward*, ed. by C. Gilbert, B. Journé, H. Laroche, C. Bieder (Springer, Cham, 2018), pp. 151–158
13. J.C. Le Coze, Vive la diversité. HRO and resilience engineering. Safety Science (2016). https://doi.org/10.1016/j.ssci.2016.04.006
14. J.C. Le Coze, How safety culture can help us think. Saf. Sci. **118**, 221–229 (2019)
15. K. Sahlin-Andersson, L. Engwall, *The Expansion of Management Knowledge. Carriers, Flows, and Sources* (Stanford Business Books, Stanford, 2002)
16. A. Sturdy, The consultancy process–an insecure business? J. Manag. Stud. **34**(3), 389–413 (1997)
17. A.J. Sturdy, K. Handley, T. Clark, R. Fincham, *Management Consultancy, Boundaries and Knowledge in Action* (Oxford University Press, Oxford, 2009)

Breaking the Glass Ceiling: Levers to Promote the Influence of Human and Organizational Factors in High-Risk Industries

Benoit Journé

Abstract A growing gap is emerging between the increase in human and organizational factors (HOF) expertise and the success of HOF operational approaches, and the rather weak influence of HOF at the strategic level of organizations. This chapter seeks to understand this paradox and identify some levers to promote HOF influence. We assume that (1) the paradox is an outcome of the "long road" of evolutions in HOF knowledge and its experts over forty years; (2) these evolutions have multiplied concepts and practices without a clear global coherence and without a political and institutional agenda; (3) breaking the HOF "glass ceiling" requires action on several levers at the conceptual level, the professional level, the management level and finally at political and institutional levels.

Keywords HOF evolution · Glass ceiling · Paradox

1 Introduction

It is now widely accepted that industrial safety is not just a question of technical design and engineering. Academics have produced a significant amount of knowledge about human and organizational factors (HOF). A set of HOF principles has been defined, and many concrete actions and programs have been successfully implemented at an operational level by emerging communities of HOF experts and practitioners.

But behind this apparent success, HOF are currently facing a challenging paradox. Indeed, even in the most advanced companies, the dramatic development of HOF knowledge and practices has not really helped to increase the influence of HOF on the strategic and management decisions that could have a significant impact on safety. In other words, a "glass ceiling" has emerged.

This lack of influence at the strategic and executive levels may have a negative feedback on HOF practices implemented at the operational level. This occurs every time a management tool is implemented, or a strategic decision is made that ignores

B. Journé (✉)
Université de Nantes, Nantes, France
e-mail: Benoit.Journe@univ-nantes.fr

B. Journé et al. (eds.), *Human and Organisational Factors*,
SpringerBriefs in Safety Management,
https://doi.org/10.1007/978-3-030-25639-5_15

or even contradicts HOF principles, meaning that HOF risk losing influence at all levels.

The key idea of this chapter is the following: breaking the glass ceiling cannot be limited to the presence of HOF experts within the board of directors. HOF influence lies in its legitimacy rooted in its expertise. HOF experts are not meant to directly participate in strategic decision-making, but could be involved in the rebuilding of a conceptual and practical coherence as well as in institutional work that could put HOF knowledge and practices at the core of strategic decision processes, management practices, management tools and operational practices.

2 The Evolution of HOF: Extending the Scope of Knowledge and the Variety of Issues

The evolution of HOF doctrines and practices shows a continuous enlargement of their scope. This has been fueled by both the analysis of normal functioning and the lessons learned from major accidents in high risk industries.

2.1 From Human-Machine Interactions and Human Error…

HOF practices are rooted in ergonomic models of people at work (physical and cognitive) in order to optimize human-machine interactions. "Human factors" and ergonomics emphasize the importance of "human errors" and the need to reduce them, at the individual level (optimization of human-machine interactions, fighting against "error inducing" designs) as well as at the collective level ("Crew Resource Management"). Such approaches still exist through "human performance" programs and best practices, but remain limited by important drawbacks caused by their "behavioral" and psychological biases.

2.2 …To Organizational Factors…

However, the concept of "human error" is not purely behavioral, cognitive or technical, it also opens the way to organizational and managerial approaches. Errors are not limited to imperfections and weaknesses that should be eradicated through intensive training, good procedures and tight management and control or moral values. Their human dimension lies in them being an integral part of the normal functioning of humans in the real world. The challenge for safety is not to suppress all forms of errors, but to use human errors to access the complexity of the risky socio-technical system that is operated [7]. Managing human errors requires both transparency (to understand what really happened) and learning processes (to prevent repetition of the same error).

The managerial implications of this assumption are crucial. Errors must be distinguished from faults or intentional violations. This evolution is based on the promotion of "just culture" as a key component of a wider "safety culture", and on the abandon of "blame culture".

Hence, blaming errors becomes a management fault that impedes transparency (increasing organizational silence) and learning processes and therefore produce negative impacts on safety.

This represents a turning-point. HOF are no longer referring only to "human factors" and instead are examining "organizational factors": safety can be negatively or positively affected by organizations and not just by people or technology. The process of "normalization of deviance" [12] demonstrated that, for example, rather than there being someone who broke the existing NASA procedures, the whole Challenger launch procedure and management practices related to decision-making deviated from safety to performance goals and "produced" the accident.

Conversely, the High Reliability Organizations theory (HRO) showed that safety is "produced" during normal functioning by specific organizational settings and processes, and by management practices and culture [8]. Safety appears to be the outcome of a "social order" [11]. The emphasis is put on the way organizations deal with competing objectives and competing professional groups.

2.3 …To Inter-organizational and Institutional Relationships

HOF have recently tackled a wider issue: the impact of inter-organizational relationships on safety. This includes relationships between licensees and subcontractors as well as between the regulator (or auditor) and licensees (or auditees) and supposes to develop a new institutional approach to safety. A lot is still to be done in this new area.

3 The Glass Ceiling Paradox of HOF: Growing Knowledge, but Weak Influence

The extension of the scope and the issues tackled by HOF represents significant progress, but also reveals a major weakness since it did not provide HOF with more influence in the decisions made by organizations. Despite the emergence of HOF networks and professional communities that implemented HOF programs at a very operational level, many HOF practitioners are aware of the weak influence HOF have on top management decisions. Our assumption is that this growing gap between knowledge and influence reveals the existence of a "glass ceiling" favorizing the rise of an organizational hypocrisy [2]. The HOF discourse about safety is totally neglected or contradicted by the board of directors and strategic decision makers when it comes to safety issues. This is a major threat because HOF may lose their legitimacy from the point of view of fieldworkers and first line managers who take a crucial part in the production of safety performances. Furthermore, the multiplication of issues tackled by HOF, may create confusion in the messages delivered to the practitioners.

4 Levers for an Influential HOF in Organizations

Several levers can be activated to break the glass ceiling and strengthen the influence and the coherence of HOF approaches all over the organization. We distinguish between academic and empirical levers, but these interact and should obviously be activated together, and the academic ones should feed several of the empirical ones.

4.1 Academic and Conceptual Levers for Multiple but Coherent HOF Research and Knowledge Integration

Academically, the first challenge is to link together human factors and organizational factors into a more integrated HOF approach. As suggested before, the evolution of HOF from human factors (micro level) to organizational factors (meso level) to inter-organizational factors (macro level) has required a multiplication of concepts, methods and models borrowed from various academic disciplines beyond ergonomics: psychology, sociology, anthropology, management, safety sciences, political sciences… Although these disciplines compete or sometimes collaborate with difficulty, it is very important to preserve this plurality of approaches to prevent the risk of over-simplification of safety and security issues.

How then to reintroduce coherence while keeping the plurality of the approaches? A limited, but strong and coherent core set of concepts bridging the micro/meso/macro levels and the various disciplines involved must be defined. We believe the concepts of "activity" and "organizing" can play this role, for a number of reasons. First, they are cross-disciplinary. Second, they can operate at human, organizational and inter-organizational levels. Third, they assume that safety is *produced* (or fails to be produced) by human "activities" and organizational processes. Focusing on "organizing" is a way to assume that organizations are continuously "happening" [10] through day-to-day activities made of decision-making, sense-making and collective discussions about the issues and difficulties practitioners and managers face to "do a good job". Fourth, they put complex tensions, contradictions and paradoxes at the core of safety issues (variety of goals and constraints; planning vs. managing the unexpected; etc.). Fifth, they share a common methodology based on direct observations of very contextualized activities that take place at various organizational and inter-organizational levels. Such observations should feed rich case studies that could be part of a science-based and facts-based approach to HOF.

Finally, building the theoretical coherence of HOF through "activity" and "organizing" is a way to create the framework for fruitful discussions between competing approaches (cf. normal functioning approach proposed by HRO vs. knowledge of accidents) and various academic disciplines. Thus, we advocate[1] for a pragmatist (Dewey) and interactionist (Goffman) approach to HOF.

4.2 Empirical Levers for Embedding HOF in Actual Organization Practices at All Levels

Some suggest that the best way to promote HOF would be to act directly at the political level, turning HOF into a business function in high-risk industries (cf. chapter "Turning the Management of Safety Risk into a Business Function: The Challenge for Industrial Sociotechnical Systems in the 21st Century" by Daniel Mauriño in this book) and/or to give a seat on the board of directors to the HOF chief executive. Would it automatically break the glass ceiling and give HOF more influence? Possible drawbacks exist. First, HOF experts may spend more time dealing with power issues rather than safety issues, fighting against the interests of other business functions and bargaining for more resources at the expenses of other functions. Second, the presence of a HOF representative on the board of directors can be useless if their voice is not heard, in case of self-censorship or if they get "captured" by others (abandoning HOF's interests and adopting others' interests). What is true for the board of directors can also appear to be true at every board or meeting, whatever their hierarchical level in the company. Therefore, it is important to legitimate the actual influence of HOF rather than their formal presence. In other words, HOF influence depends more on being active in "organizing" processes than being present in formal "organization".

We assume that HOF influence at the highest levels is a combination of legitimacy, management principles, concrete management tools and organizational settings that support the diffusion of HOF expertise across business functions and hierarchical levels, inside the organization but also outside, in relation with key stakeholders. HOF legitimacy comes from their expertise, derived from academic research, but also from the existence of more or less formal professional communities of HOF experts and practitioners and their reflexivity [5]. Such communities elaborate strong professional cultures that include safety as part of "doing a good job". But HOF experts, professional communities and safety cultures need management support to spread their influence from the bottom to the top of the organization. This is where management principles, management tools and organizational settings come into play.

[1] In Foncsi but also in Chaire RESOH, a research project dedicated to HOF in inter-organizational safety issues (IMT-Atlantique, Andra, IRSN, Naval group, Orano).

The coherence of HOF management tools (i.e. formal safety culture of the company, performance indicators, pre-job briefing…) and their connections with management tools used by other functions is a key issue and requires specific engineering to prevent cacophony and promote polyphony [4]. This is especially the case with Human Resources (competency, career, salary, social relations…), management control (industrial and financial performance reporting tools) and with higher hierarchical levels. HOF expertise may irrigate the organization through these interconnected management tools that embed various visions of "doing a good job". Management processes are in place to enable discussions on professional activities and difficulties with safety issues to be organized. Designing and managing discussion spaces [3, 9] is a management responsibility. Then subsidiary management becomes the key principle to organize the connection of hierarchical levels through the different discussion spaces. It is also a way to make strategic managers and CEO feel really responsible for safety and to include it in strategic discussions.

Since the top management levels and strategy oversee the relationships with the organization's environment, breaking the glass ceiling by addressing the top management levels with HOF expertise and safety issues, supposes to put them at the core of the dialog with external stakeholders. It is especially the case for the regulator and for the "civil society" that have important expectations about safety, security and transparency. At a strategic level, safety is *produced* through such dialogs that have to be engineered.

Finally, the activation of the empirical levers we have identified requires "institutional work" [1, 6] realized by HOF experts and managers at various levels as a way of building HOF legitimacy and putting HOF expertise with the right shape, at the right time, in the right place to make the right decisions.

References

1. A. Berger-Sabbatel, B. Journé, Organizing risk communication for effective preparedness: using plans as a catalyst for risk communication, in *Risk Communication for the Future*, ed. by M. Bourrier, C. Bieder (Springer, Cham, 2018), pp. 31–44
2. N. Brunsson, *The Organization of Hypocrisy: Talk, Decisions and Actions in Organizations* (Wiley, 1989)
3. M. Detchessahar, B. Journé, Managing strategic discussions in organizations: a Habermasian perspective. M@n@gement **21**(2), 773–802 (2018)
4. M. Detchessahar, S. Gentil, A. Grevin, B. Journé, Entre cacophonie et silence organisationnel, concevoir le dialogue sur le travail. Le cas de projets de maintenance dans une industrie à risque. Annales des Mines-Gérer et comprendre (130), 33–45 (2017)
5. J. Lave, E. Wenger, *Situated Learning. Legitimate Peripheral Participation* (Cambridge University Press, Cambridge, 1991)
6. T. Lawrence, R. Suddaby, B. Leca, *Institutional Work: Actors and Agency in Institutional Studies of Organizations* (Cambridge University Press, 2009)
7. J. Reason, The identification of latent organizational failures in complex systems, in *Verification and Validation of Complex Systems: Human Factors Issues*, ed. by J.A. Wise, V.D. Hopkin, P. Stager (Springer, Berlin, Heidelberg, Germany, 1993), pp. 223–237

8. K.H. Roberts, Some characteristics of one type of high reliability organization. Organ. Sci. **1**(2), 160–176 (1990)
9. R. Rocha, V. Mollo, F. Daniellou, Work debate spaces: a tool for developing a participatory safety management. Appl. Ergon. **46**, 107–114 (2015)
10. T.R. Schatzki, On organizations as they happen. Organ. Stud. **27**(12), 1863–1873 (2006)
11. P.R. Schulman, The negotiated order of organizational reliability. Adm. Soc. **25**(3), 353–372 (1993)
12. D. Vaughan, *The Challenger Launch Decision: Risky Technology, Culture and Deviance at NASA* (University of Chicago Press, Chicago, USA, 1996)

HOF: Adjusting the Rule-Based Safety/Managed Safety Balance and Keeping Pace with a Changing Reality

Caroline Kamaté

Abstract It is commonly acknowledged among at-risk industrial sectors that improvement in safety performance requires better consideration of HOF. Tensions and even contradictions exist between work and organisation as theoretically understood, and the reality of the shop floor, with its constraints, its power games and more. HOF specialists are, in some ways, the voice of reality in complex sociotechnical systems such as at-risk organisations. The HOF approach provides, at all levels, 'adjustment loops' to promote safe and efficient human activity and contribute to the business whole performance. However, the way HOF are structured varies widely depending on organisations and the expectations in terms of both impact and sustainability are not always met. This final chapter briefly summarizes and discusses some of the axes for improvement previously presented in the book.

Keywords Reality · 'Organising' · HOF dynamic loop

1 Introduction

It is nowadays generally accepted that if the safety strategy of a company is to be improved, a further step must be taken in the consideration of human and organisational factors (HOF). Thus, requests on the topic of HOF abound. However, the way HOF structures are organised denotes a heterogenous and fragmented HOF landscape, according to the company and even within companies. Furthermore, what is implemented does not always meet the expectations in terms of impact and continuity, hence the safety outcomes, and HOF actors sometimes deplore a lack of leeway and integration of their contribution at the organisation's highest levels.

Thus, although (almost) everybody is convinced about the importance of considering human and organisational factors for safety, in most industries there is a feeling of dissatisfaction or even frustration. What are the conceptual, structural and func-

C. Kamaté (✉)
FonCSI, Toulouse, France
e-mail: caroline.kamate@foncsi.org

B. Journé et al. (eds.), *Human and Organisational Factors*,
SpringerBriefs in Safety Management,
https://doi.org/10.1007/978-3-030-25639-5_16

tional levers for an implementation of HOF approaches that efficiently contribute to safety performance? Based on the work presented in the previous chapters of the book, this synthesis is an attempt to summarize and build on the main findings.

2 HOF Approaches for Capturing Reality

Adopting a HOF approach means examining human work within the organisation, notably beyond the framework, rules and procedures that govern it. Indeed, beyond the prescriptions, depending on the context and its unforeseen circumstances, employees adapt their activity, which is not limited to the prescribed work, to 'do their job'. In the same way, the organisation is above all a structure, with an organisation chart and rules which frame its functioning as well as accounts that must be rendered to the external stakeholders. But an organisation is also a process, it is continuously under construction: it is the living and dynamic product of a set of interactions and social regulations. It is the outcome of an actual 'organising' work carried out daily by all actors, including managers through the arbitrations they are led to do. This organising is both vertical (between hierarchical levels) and horizontal (management of internal and external interfaces).

This hiatus between a theoretical and normative view of how work should be done or how organisations should function, and what really goes on in situation, is at the core of HOF. HOF specialists have the duty to always consider reality and its constraints, and to 'ring the reality bell' at all levels of the organisation. They may somehow be considered as 'providers of reality'.

3 Support 'Organising'

There are some essential conditions for allowing HOF people to fulfill their functional mission. They must be connected to the shop floor and be able to feed back reality of work to the highest levels of the organisation. This means their words must not be censured, and managers should also be open to listen to bad news. The freedom of speech of HOF people is a number one priority and must be protected. HOF resources must be deployed wherever needed in the organisation to identify contradictory issues and support managers in their arbitrations and trade-offs to get the job done, and to promote interactions at all levels. Thus, they favorize constant 'organising'.

4 Work on the Gap between Expectations and Responses

The way HOF specialists and senior managers respectively think about HOF, leads to differences in their perception of the role of HOF specialists. There is often a gap between some normative expectations of industry consisting in operational recommendations, quick and limited in scope interventions, and responses from HOF actors, both academics and practitioners, that are not that 'simple' … As an example, if some human factors at the workplace level can quite easily be monitored by indicators, this is generally not the case anymore when the perimeter is extended to the level of the organisation, even more so with a changing dimension.

HOF specialists claim that an organisation is a socio-technical system with some human and organisational dimensions that mainly escape monitoring by indicators. Moreover, industrial companies, like other complex systems, are basically unstable. But despite the discourses about the impact of human and organisational factors and their hardly quantifiable features, for most company leaders, the organisation is seen above all as a techno-economic system, and it is mainly as such that they 'work it out'. They perceive the role of HOF specialists as being precisely to provide sociotechnical engineering, and not to remind them how difficult it is to do so. HOF are expected to restore a regulated safety ensuring 'normal stable' operations. Most regulators support this vision too, because it is easier to control and display, and reassuring for public opinion.

On this basis, there is de facto unrest among HOF specialists, and frustration from both sides. Since they cannot really fulfil the promise of socio-technical engineering, they eventually could be seen in a position of a 'permanently failing function'. However, they offer an 'imperfect remedy' for an 'imperfect reality', and they must constantly get back to work because this is a never-ending mission.

5 Rebalance the O within the F

Although internal HOF structures regularly identify organisational causes when analysing unwanted events, they usually have much more influence on human factors than on organisational ones. There are several reasons that can explain this situation. One is the profile of HOF specialists—mostly ergonomists and psychologists—and their scope of intervention which is sometimes limited to health, safety and working conditions. Within that field, their expertise is fully recognized and the methods and tools they provide are operational and have proved efficient. However, work on organisational factors seems to remain within the purview of a different category of actors, mainly management specialists, who, unlike most HOF specialists who work in close interaction with front-line managers, operate at the decision-making level. To some extent, HOF specialists face a 'glass ceiling' that prevent them accessing the strategic levels of the company. This might undermine the efficiency of their approach due to their scope of action being limited to one part of the problem, and could significantly weaken their influence on strategic decisions. Unlocking this situation requires working at both conceptual and practical levels, starting with building a more integrated and consistent approach towards HOF around the cross-disciplinary concept of 'organising'. Promoting training of both executive committee members on the basis of HOF and HOF people in risk management, plus the presence of HOF experts within the executive board to provide support for decision-makers by forming binomen for example, are promising levers for safety and performance because they promote the reconciliation of these two worlds.

6 Safety Alone Is not the Key

Companies do not have only safety to manage and the priority given to safety does not always translate into reality. And, although this is a slight exaggeration, HOF can be described as knowledge-oriented while managers are solution-oriented. Consequently, at first glance HOF is not an issue for managers and must therefore be turned into a managerial issue (design, productivity…). Thus, to better mobilize around HOF, it is of strategic importance to demonstrate the connection of HOF to other key dimensions of business performance and to overall risk management rather than to safety only. The purpose of implementing HOF approaches is to promote safe and efficient human activity. But beyond safety and human efficiency, better consideration of HOF fosters the whole industrial performance through the integrative function of human activity. It also leads to the limitation of costs like human cost for performance (incidents or accidents, exhaustion, demobilization), costs due to late identification and catch up of design errors… Rather than the safety one, hanging this banner might give HOF people better chance to get attention from top managers. Once 'inoculated', once convinced sometimes by leading examples, the will of a few top-managers might facilitate openness to HOF from the whole organisation and support from the direction. The HOF policy must then translate into strategic piloting tools and the deployment of HOF resources all along the organisation's key processes.

7 Reinforce the Dialogue around HOF with External Stakeholders

Depending on the industrial sector, consideration of HOF by the regulators varies widely, with the authorities supervising civil aviation probably the more advanced in that field. There is no doubt that the greater incorporation of HOF into the regulatory framework is a powerful lever for improving their consideration by companies, and therefore promoting efficient and sustainable HOF approaches. Nevertheless, the risk exists of becoming too prescriptive and of shifting too much towards the rule-based safety side, thus denaturing the very purpose of HOF which is to look beyond the rules. The emphasis should be placed on the need for industrial organisations and regulators to share HOF fundamentals and engage a discussion.

Better knowledge and acknowledgment of HOF by judges is also a paramount issue in view of the increasing judicialization of industrial disasters. This is reflected by the good reception given by the European Parliament to the concept of just culture in civil aviation.

More globally, better consideration of HOF in inter-organisational relationships requires an institutional work which represents a promising area for renewed safety approaches.

8 Assume the Dual Objective of HOF Structuring

The way HOF are structured in a company must serve objectives of two different natures. HOF must be well structured to achieve their primary functional purpose as reality sensors which largely consists in managing the gaps between the work as it is conceived and the work as it is done, and seeking to narrow the gap. For that purpose, HOF must be networked and finely inserted in processes where safety is 'manufactured'. Nevertheless, HOF structure also has a symbolic scope. Internally, it positions HOF within the organisation's culture, establishing the permanence of the HOF approach, its relevance and legitimacy. Regarding the external environment of the company, it stresses the importance given to safety, designates the stakeholders' interlocutors and publicizes compliance with explicit or implicit standards. This symbolic role requires a much more visible and homogenous structuration. The risk exists that company leaders, in their arbitrations, emphasise the symbolic role because it is more visible and appears the most 'profitable' in the short term. But they need to adopt both strategies and assume this duality. The idea is to use the symbolic structure as an entry and exit point, providing a framework to the functional role of HOF, the stake being that HOF people can operate, benefiting from the resources and leeway they need.

9 The HOF Virtuous Loop

The importance of overcoming old models essentially based on rule-based safety is nowadays more widely acknowledged. Since hazardous industries, like any other complex systems, are dynamic and unstable socio-technical systems, the largest potential for progression lies on the side of managed safety, which could also be named initiative-based safety. By starting from the real work with emphasis on 'organising', HOF approaches promote, at all levels, 'loops of adjustment' between the top managerial models and the reality of work. By identifying paradoxes and supporting the consideration of the different points of view, the HOF loop seeks to turn tensions into opportunities for improvement, rather than becoming sources of blockage. The instability of industrial organisations must be accepted in order to anticipate and adapt to future changes. Uncertainty, risk and a certain incompleteness contribute to adaptation, while trying to find fixed solutions carries the risk for organisations of always fall behind the times in a constantly changing world. Thus, rather than aiming to achieve perfection at a given moment, the HOF loop participates in considering imperfection as an asset rather than a problem, therefore contributing to organisational agility.

To keep the HOF loop dynamic and successful, HOF specialists face great challenges. They must provide advice and support at the highest level of the organisation, while keeping in touch with the reality of the shop floor. Being close both to decision-makers and to the workplace, maintaining the same interest for the work of all those who contribute to safety and the same quality of dialogue requires them to master different languages. They have to make decisions about the right battles to be fought, which managers should be supported in their arbitrations and which resources must be negotiated. Their voice is essential and must weigh in the conduct of technical and organisational changes. And, of course, they must continuously stay up-to-date with advances in cognitive, social and organisational sciences. All of this requires the top management to be open to HOF and to unconditionally support implementation of a consistent HOF approach.

www.ingramcontent.com/pod-product-compliance
Lightning Source LLC
LaVergne TN
LVHW082349200926
848481LV00012B/3506